This book is dedicated to the late Lloyd "Muggs" Webb. When I began clowning and was struggling to learn more, Muggs took me under his wing and helped me more than he ever knew. He has earned my unwavering gratitude.

Table of Contents

Preface

Planning to be a clown at a school or church carnival? Preparing for Halloween or a party? Dressing up to perform as a children's entertainer? These are common reasons to dress up like a clown. Yet many people simply dress up but they really don't look like clowns. Looking like a real clown takes a certain degree of knowledge and skill.

The most noticeable aspect of clowning is the clown's characteristic appearance. Clowns are identified and distinguished by their colorful costumes and makeup. If you want to look like a *real* clown, you will need to learn the proper procedures of makeup application.

Whether you plan to simply dress up for a school or church event or have desires to perform as a clown, you should look the part. Many novice clowns, not knowing better, use lipstick and street makeup to draw large eyes and a mouth on their faces. The end result is often grotesque and may even frighten children.

Even an untrained eye can easily distinguish the face of an amateur clown from that of a professional. The professional clown face is evenly balanced, color coordinated, complementary to the clown's natural facial features, and pleasing to look at. The unknowledgable amateur's is not. Although you may not have plans on becoming a professional clown, you certainly want to look like one — and can with the proper knowledge and a little practice.

When I began clowning a number of years ago very little printed material was available on the subject of clown makeup application. In those days most clowns considered their craft a trade secret and if they passed on the information, they would only do so verbally. Information published on the subject was either sketchy or of questionable worth.

Since that time, several works have been published which have included information on how to apply makeup. But until now, no book has been devoted exclusively to clown makeup design and application.

Many important areas of clown makeup have been overlooked in previous works. This unique book offers complete details on powdering the makeup, an essential but often overlooked procedure needed to obtain a professional appearance. Information is included on how to apply rubber, foam, and putty noses, as well how to properly handle eyeglasses, beards, mustaches, wigs and skull caps. Lining techniques, which make the facial features sharp and bold, are clearly explained. Also included are instructions for applying the live eye to enhance animation. An entire chapter treats makeup problems and how to correct them, as well as methods of makeup removal.

In order to give a broad view of makeup techniques, two other award winning clowns, Delores Rademaker and Jack Anderson, demonstrate their methods of makeup application. The step-by-step series of photographs that accompany the text show in detail how to create a professional looking clown face.

I recommend that you read the entire book before attempting to design your own clown face. You will need to know, or at least be aware of, the information contained in most all of the chapters before you can properly design and apply a good looking clown face. Makeup application itself, is relatively easy. The most difficult task is designing a clown face that enhances your own natural features and is pleasing in apperance.

While this book is primarily written to help beginning clowns learn the basics of makeup application, it can also benefit the seasoned clown who is looking for new and better ways to apply makeup.

In this book you will learn the secrets of the trade that in times past were reserved only for professional clowns. With this knowledge you will be able to create a unique and pleasing clown face of your own.

Jim Roberts

Chapter One

Clown Types

Clowns commonly belong to one of three types. They differ in facial makeup, costuming, and in the way they behave. The three categories are the whiteface, the auguste, and the tramp.

The whiteface is at the top of the clown hierarchy in regards to physical skill and intelligence. He is the straight man while the auguste plays more of a slapstick role. If Bud Abbott and Lou Costello had been clowns, Abbott would have been the whiteface and the comic Costello, the auguste. The tramp clown is at the bottom of the clown pecking order and will be the recipient of an auguste's jokes.

WHITEFACE

The whiteface clown dates back to the mid 1700s. His makeup, as the name implies, consists of a white base coat with brightly colored features and markings or accents.

Neat Whiteface

There are two generally recognized types of whiteface clowns. One, which evolved from the European influence, is referred to as the *neat whiteface*. It is sometimes called the *pierrot whiteface* after the French clown Pierrot. The neat whiteface's makeup has simple features. The accent colors are red and black. The mouth is relatively small, normally no larger than the clown's natural lips. The tip of the nose may be painted red, but the clown wears no false nose. A skullcap, a stocking like topping which covers all the hair, usually tops the neat whiteface's head. April Glaros shown in Figure 1-1 is a typical neat whiteface.

Comedy Whiteface

Sometimes called the *grotesque whiteface*, the comedy whiteface has developed in the last half century. Like the neat whiteface, this clown also has a base coat of white makeup, but the features

Figure 1-1 Neat whiteface.

Figure 1-2
Comedy whiteface.

on the comedy whiteface are larger and bolder. The comedy whiteface may also use accent colors other than just red and black. The nose can be either painted on or false. Comedy whiteface clowns are more slapstick than the neat whiteface and tend to have a character closer to the auguste.

The comedy whiteface normally wears a brightly colored wig. However, a few will wear a skullcap. Like the neat whiteface, the comedy whiteface covers all skin, either by makeup, head covering, or costume. Marcela "Mama Clown" Murad, shown in Figure 1-2, is a typical comedy whiteface.

AUGUSTE CLOWN

Unlike the whiteface clowns, the base coat for the auguste clown is a flesh or pink color. White is only applied around the mouth and the eyes. Features and accents are bolder than those worn by the whiteface clown, and accent colors are more varied. Most auguste clowns have large red lips though black lips are also acceptable for the auguste. In keeping with the outlandish features, the auguste will normally wear a false nose and a brightly colored wig.

The auguste clown is a slapstick clown and is the one who normally takes the pie in the face or the bucket of water from the whiteface. This clown portrays a character less intelligent and more clumsy than the whiteface. Georgia "Shananigns" Morris, an auguste clown, is shown in Figure 1-3.

TRAMP CLOWN

The third type of clown is the tramp. This clown has black, brown, or dark gray whiskers, a large white mouth, rosy cheeks, a red nose, and white

Figure 1-3 Auguste clown.

Figure 1-4 Happy hobo.

Figure 1-5 Sad tramp.

around the eyes. The remainder of the face should look suntanned to suggest the outdoor lifestyle of a hobo or tramp.

The tramp clowns as we now know them derived their appearance from hobos who rode the rails back in the days of the depression. During these excursions, the soot from the steam engine would leave a deposit on the whisker stubble, thus the appearance of a dark beard. The rider of the rails would wipe his mouth with the back of his hand or cuff of his coat to remove soot from his mouth when he ate. This area showed up as white compared to the soot covered stubble. Thus the white mouth is used. Similarly, wiping "sleep" from his eyes led to the clowns' use of a white area around each eye.

A brown, black, or gray wig is normally worn by both the hobo and traditional tramp. However, some wear no wig, letting their natural hair show, but this should be only if the clown's natural hair fits the character.

The tramp is at the bottom of the clown ladder. He is the butt of all jokes. The auguste will give the tramp the pie in the face or toss on him the bucket of water.

Happy Hobo

Two types of tramp character are generally seen. The first has the happy-go-lucky attitude, and is sometimes referred to as a happy hobo. Red Skelton's character, Freddy the Freeloader, is an example of a happy hobo. Freddy is poor but he does not mind. He sees a pot of gold at the end of every rainbow. The hobo may have a happy or neutral mouth as shown by Bill "Boho" Rayner in Figure 1-4. His clothes, although tattered, usually have a cared for look. Patches have been applied over holes and rips have been sewn together. Bright colors are sometimes used for patching material.

Traditional Tramp

The traditional tramp has a sad disposition. Nothing will turn out right for him regardless of what he does. Though he seldom smiles he accepts his station in life. Emmett Kelly is probably the most famous of all tramp clowns. His clothes are the standard for the traditional tramp. They are literally rags, and no attempt has been made to repair them. While a person may laugh at or with a hobo, they will feel pity toward the tramp. Bill Lozon in Figure 1-5 is a typical traditional tramp.

Chapter Two

Makeup Materials

GREASEPAINT

Greasepaint, also known as *cream foundation*, is the material used to cover the face in making the transition to a clown. Cosmetic makeup, while okay for modeling and normal wear, will not hold up under the long hours and sometimes extremely warm conditions experienced in clowning. Lipstick or paints should never be used.

Water based clown makeups are also available. While these may be slightly easier to apply, do not use them. They will run when exposed to moisture, whether it be perspiration, rain, or a glass of water in the face. For a top quality makeup job greasepaint should be used.

Greasepaint can be purchased in cake, stick, or semi-liquid forms. The varieties differ in consistency, with the stick being the stiffest or most solid of the three. Some sticks are packaged in

a cardboard tube and are wrapped in waxed paper. Other sticks are packaged in oversized lipstick type plastic containers.

The cake form is supplied in small tubs and can be applied to the face with finger tips, makeup sponges, or brushes. If the makeup in cake form is too stiff to apply with a brush, it may be softened by adding a drop or two of baby oil which is thoroughly mixed with the greasepaint.

The semi-liquid has about the consistency of toothpaste and is packaged in a collapsible tube like toothpaste. It is easily applied with a brush, but is difficult to powder without smearing.

A beginning clown should use the cake makeup, waiting until he or she becomes more experienced before trying the stick or semi-liquid.

Figure 2-1 shows some of the makeup materials commonly used by clowns.

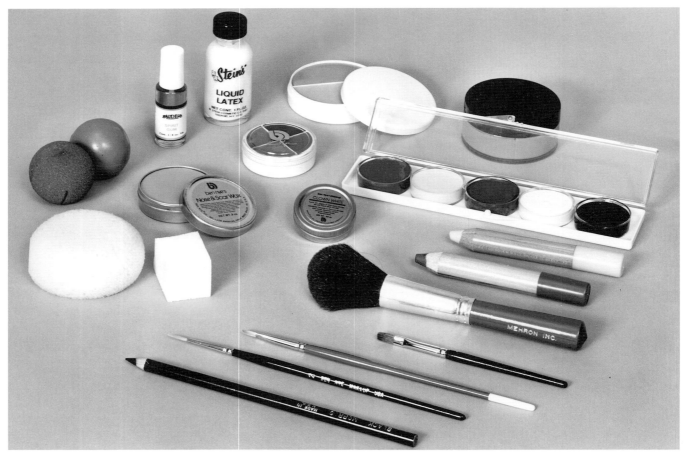

Figure 2-1 Makeup supplies.

Brands of Makeup

Although cosmetic makeup such as Revlon and Maybelline are used to a limited extent, good quality theatrical makeup is the standard. The many brands of makeup on the market range from excellent to poor in terms of quality. If you use a cheap or substandard makeup, you cannot expect to have the best possible appearance no matter how well you have applied it. I would recommend four brands which are most popular with clowns. They are Mehron, Kryolan, Ben Nye, and Bob Kelly. Other good theatrical makeups comomonly used are Stein, Playbill, and Zauder. These brands are available from most theatrical and novelty shops.

LINING MATERIAL

All clowns apply lines to their faces. These lines are either decorative, or are used to outline certain features such as the red lips. These lines can be applied one of several ways:

• With a liner pencil such as Maybelline brand.
• With a china marker grease pencil.
• With liquid eyeliner such as Maybelline brand.
• With black greasepaint applied with a sable liner brush.

The liner pencil and china marker are easier to use than the liquid liner, but they do not show up as brightly.

MAKEUP SUPPLIES

In addition to the makeup, several other items are necessary before the application can begin. A complete list includes:

- Greasepaint or cream foundations (predominant colors are white, pink or flesh, red, black, and blue).
- A makeup sponge for the application of clown white or other base coat materials.
- A liner pencil such as those made by Playbill and Maybelline, or liquid eyeliner and a liner brush.
- A ¼ inch, and ⅜ inch brush for application of greasepaint to the face. Sable brushes are a bit more expensive than others, but are worth the price.
- A white liner pencil such as Playbill, and a pencil sharpener.
- A white cotton sock filled with a good grade talcum powder, or a powder puff and talcum powder. Any brand of powder will work but avoid talcum powders containing cornstarch.
- A 1½ inch soft bristled paint brush, makeup brush, sheepskin powder puff, or shaving brush to remove excess powder.
- A small foam makeup sponge for removal of heavy powder deposits.
- A head band or stocking cap to keep hair away from the face while applying makeup.
- Facial tissue, paper towels, baby wipes, or cotton swabs to remove smeared greasepaint or misapplications.
- A sponge or a spray mist bottle to dampen the face after applying powder.
- Latex, silicone, or spirit gum adhesive for the attachment of an artificial nose. Also adhesive dissolver or remover. Surgical adhesive is excellent for sensitive skins.
- Baby oil, baby shampoo, or cold cream for the removal of greasepaint.

MAKEUP KIT

A makeup kit is a collection of makeup, brushes, fake noses, and other items, housed in a container for storage and transportation. Cosmetic manufacturers sometimes sell special boxes designed to hold their own products and, although these are usually very good, they are comparatively expensive. Many other, and cheaper, types of containers can be used to carry your makeup supplies. Train cases, fishing tackle boxes, and sewing kit containers are the most commonly used to hold makeup supplies.

Some clowns keep a variety of items other than makeup supplies in their kits. Common additions are safety pins, aspirin, mirrors, and mouthwash.

The author's makeup kit is small, containing only the necessities. The advantage of a compact kit is that it will fit into a six-pack cooler, where it will remain cool on a hot days.

Chapter Three

Designing a Clown Face

Designing a good clown face is one of the most difficult parts in creating a professional looking clown character. Long after learning how to apply the makeup, you may still be making slight adjustments to the design of your face. Even professional clowns continue to make adjustments to their facial design after settling on a basic pattern.

The most important concept you must learn in designing your own clown face is that the purpose of clown makeup is *not* to paint a mask over your face. Makeup should be used to *enhance and magnify your natural facial expressions.*

Modern clown facial designs were developed in the circuses before electronic voice amplification was used. Since audiences were a great distance from the performers, clowns had to communicate by movement and expression.

Because their expressions had to be seen from a distance, facial features were exaggerated.

Professional clowns learned that the most effective features are those that are designed to amplify facial movement. When a clown shows emotion, it is easily seen in the face. A good clown face will be designed so that it will move with the facial muscles to exaggerate facial expressions. This will give the clown a life-like or animated appearance.

Since the eyes and mouth are the most expressive parts of the face, the lips and eyebrows are made larger than life to draw people's attention to them. The areas around the eyes and mouth are also the areas of the face in which we can control the movements. In addition to opening and closing the eyes and the mouth, muscles allow us to raise and lower the eyebrows, to frown, or laugh. Combined with accent markings the makeup design helps exaggerate the movements.

The three basic features used in designing a clown face are the mouth, eyes, and nose. Each of these parts is described in detail in Chapters 8, 9, and 10. Although this chapter will explain some basic concepts you need to know in creating a good looking clown character, you should read these chapters before attempting to design your own clown face.

CHOOSING DESIGNS

When creating your face, the designs you use should (1) amplify your expressions, (2) fit the bone structure of your natural face, (3) be balanced and unified, resulting in a pleasant-looking face, and (4) define the character you portray.

One of the first things you need to do before you try to design your clown face is to look in the mirror and analyze your own natural face. Look at its shape, bone structure, and natural lines. Is your face long and thin, or full and round? What size is your mouth? Are your eyes close set or wide apart? Study the natural lines and wrinkles in your face. Make facial expressions—smile, laugh, frown, show surprise and remorse—in order to bring out your facial lines. Which lines were most prominent? What part of your face moved the most? These are the questions you should answer before you design your clown face.

To help give you some ideas on the type of features you could use, look carefully at the photographs of clowns in this book. Study the way their faces are designed. Examine pictures of clowns from other sources as well. Which features are attractive and intriguing? Which features would fit your face? Be creative and come up with some original patterns.

Looking at other clowns is a good way to get ideas, but don't copy another clown's face. A clown's face is an identifying trademark, and *no two designs* should be exactly alike.

Clown Makeup Charts

Using the makeup charts on pages 20, 21, and 22 can help you design your clown face. Make photocopies of the chart which best matches your natural facial shape and use these to create several different clown faces.

Before attempting to design a clown face, you must first decide which of the three types of clowns you want to portray: auguste, whiteface, or tramp. Once you have made your decision, you can begin to consider the many possibilities within the bounds of your chosen clown category.

Keep in mind as you design your face that, as a general rule, for whiteface and auguste clowns—the larger or more outlandish the facial features, the more slapstick the character. A skillful intelligent whiteface will have small pleasing features. A boisterous clumsy auguste will typically have large silly features.

Take a pencil and the photocopies of the makeup chart and go to a mirror. Study your face in the mirror, making note of your bone structure, facial lines, and wrinkles. As accurately as possible, draw the most prominent lines on the makeup charts. With the charts as guides, use colored pencils to compose several different clown faces to suit your personal style and the clown type you have chosen. Begin with the most important features first, the mouth and eyes. Reserve the nose and accents for last. Draw as accurately as possible, using proper colors and outlining. Try several types of eye and mouth designs; be creative and use a design you haven't seen before. Make sure that the mouth and eyes complement each other and are well balanced.

This exercise is only intended to narrow down the possibilities in your makeup design. Often a facial design that looks good on paper will look

CLOWN MAKEUP CHART
Full Face

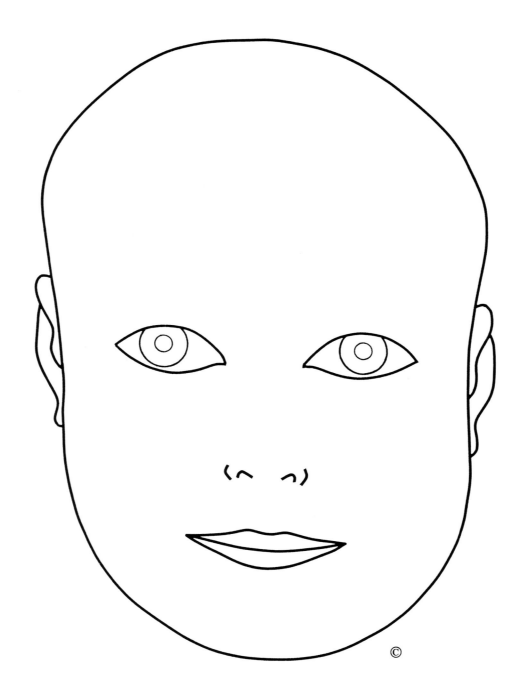

Clown Character_____

Base Color_____

Hair Style & Color_____

Notes:_____

_____

_____

_____

_____

CLOWN MAKEUP CHART
Medium Face

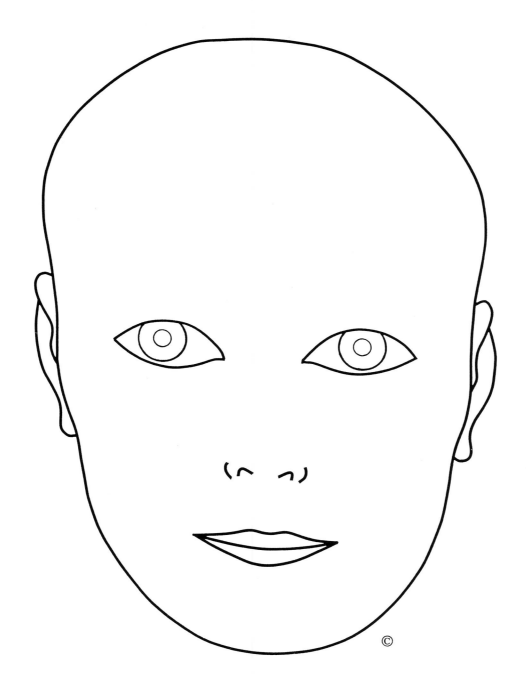

Clown Character_____   Notes:_____

Base Color_____   _____

Hair Style & Color_____   _____

This page may be reproduced for private use without further written
permission from the publisher. Mass reproduction for sale or free
distribution is prohibited under the copyright of this book.

_____

_____

CLOWN MAKEUP CHART
Thin Face

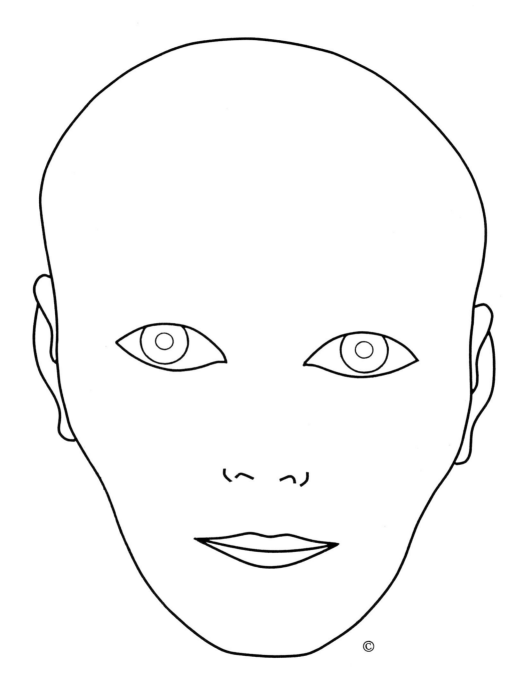

Clown Character_____

Base Color_____

Hair Style & Color_____

Notes:_____

_____

_____

_____

_____

terrible when actually applied to the face. This does not mean the design was bad, only that it does not fit your bone structure, facial shape, or facial lines. It may not be a balanced face. The same makeup design, however, might be ideal for someone with different facial features. It will be necessary for you to experiment in order to design a face that suits you.

Visual Overlay

Another method that can help you design a clown face would be to use a visual overlay. You will need an 8 x 10 inch black and white photograph of your face, several 8 x 10 inch clear or matt sheets of acetate, acrylic paint in assorted colors or Prismacolor pencils, and some artist's brushes. The acetate, paints, and colored pencils are available anywhere art or drafting supplies are sold.

Instead of using the clown makeup charts you would use the photograph of yourself. Place a clear sheet of acetate over the photograph and secure it in place with a couple of short strips of tape. Using the acrylic paint and paint brushes, paint your proposed clown face on to the overlay (Figure 3-1). If you prefer to work with dry coloring material you could use Prismacolor pencils on matt-finish acetate. Use several sheets of acetate and experiment with different clown face designs.

Using a visual overlay you can incorporate your natural facial features and shape into the design. Your sketches will show a relatively accurate picture of how your proposed clown face will actually look. Like the clown makeup charts, however, a design that looks good on paper may not necessarily look good on your face. Keep experimenting.

Apply the Designs

Going through these exercises with the clown makeup charts or the visual overlays will help you to find a suitable design complementary to your natural face.

Once you have found a few facial designs that are pleasing to you, try to reconstruct them

Figure 3-1 Using a visual overlay to design a clown face.

on your face using the makeup techniques discussed in this book. You may omit the powdering step (powdering is described in Chapter 4) when you do this to cut down on application time and to make cleanup easier.

Have a photo taken of the faces which are most pleasing to you. These photos will serve as permanent records of how the designs actually looked on your face. Examining several photos together will help you determine which face or features look best on you and which one best magnifies your expressions. This entire process can be repeated as often as necessary until you have found a clown face you are happy with.

In time, you will no longer need to rely so much on sketches for assistance but will be able to experiment with new designs by applying makeup directly on your face. As you gain more experience in applying makeup, you will alter your design slightly from time to time in a continuing effort to improve it.

FACIAL BALANCE

In order to have a pleasant looking clown face you must balance all the features. The white around the eyes should be in balance with the white of the mouth for the auguste or tramp face. Terry "Beemer" Bloes in Figure 3-2 shows a good balance of white at the eyes and mouth, as well as a properly sized nose. The whiteface clown should also balance the eyes and mouth, with little open space. Lloyd "Muggs" Webb in Figure 3-3 uses a pink muzzle to break up the open white space of his face. The nose should be sized to balance the eyes and mouth. A smaller nose must be used if your eyes are close set.

You should not use a lot of extra designs on the face such as stars, hearts, or rainbows. These are difficult to apply and do not add to the layout of the face.

Daisy's face (Figure 6-21) shows a good balance of white around the eyes with the white around the mouth. Making one area larger than the other would destroy the balance.

The white on Freckles' face (Figure 5-21) also shows balance. The eyebrows and the

Figure 3-2

Figure 3-3

mouth balance, and the red freckles reduce the look of emptiness on the face without the addition of stars, hearts, or other clutter. The nose complements the other facial features.

Strutter's tramp character (Figure 7-19) shows a well-balanced face with the white at the eyes offsetting the white at the mouth.

IMPROVE THE DESIGN

After some practice, you will decide on a design that's right for you. Go with that design, but don't be afraid to make modifications. Continue to experiment with your clown face until you are satisfied with the results. The biggest design changes or modifications will happen early in the design stage, and later changes will normally be smaller and more subtle.

Each time you change the design of your face, have someone take a photograph of you wearing the new makeup and keep it as a record. Also, put a photo of your clown face in your makeup kit to serve as a model when you next apply your makeup.

Another way to improve your design is to have a clown who is knowledgeable about makeup application and design critique your clown face. You may be surprised how a simple recommendation to add a line here or there can improve your design.

The clown face you develop should fit with the character you plan to portray. For example, you should not want to be a silent clown if you use an auguste face with large bold features. Such a clown is expected to be loud and boisterous. On the other hand, a neat whiteface clown or a sad tramp could easily fit the character of a silent clown.

And finally, do not copy another clown's face. You may pattern your eyes after one clown's design, your mouth after another, and nose after another. But, the final design should be *yours*.

Chapter Four

Basic Application Techniques

This chapter presents a brief overview of the steps necessary to properly apply makeup. Included are special notes for people who have beards and mustaches and full details on powdering. Powdering is one of the secrets of good makeup application and a step many beginners overlook.

Although this chapter explains each step in makeup application, you should read the detailed step-by-step directions contained in Chapters 5, 6, and 7 before attempting to put on makeup for the first time.

PREPARING THE FACE

Before makeup can be applied, the face must be prepared to receive the makeup. First, all cosmetic makeup must be removed. If not removed, it will mix with the clown makeup, affecting the color in the finished product.

Men who shave regularly should shave within an hour before the application of makeup. Makeup is difficult to apply over the slightest stubble. If you apply makeup to a beard or a mustache, facial hair should be recently shampooed, or the makeup will not adhere to it.

After removing cosmetic makeup, shaving, or shampooing facial hair, thoroughly wash the face with soap and water to remove all salts and oils from the skin. Salts and oils make application more difficult and cause the makeup to break down and need repair.

Cold Cream
Some sources recommend the use of a light coat of cold cream on the face before applying makeup. This, they claim, will fill open pores or smooth out rough skin. Few clowns, however, use cold cream prior to applying makeup. If it is

used on a young smooth skin, the makeup is very difficult to pat out and keep from streaking. If it is used on an older or rougher skin, repowdering is required sooner.

The argument that cold cream fills open pores or creases holds some merit, but these open pores will fill with makeup within a short period of time after application anyway.

Mirror and Lighting
Good lighting and a good mirror are essential to proper makeup application. It is extremely difficult to do a good job of makeup application in a dimly lit location. Some clowns use a makeup mirror and sit at a table to apply their makeup. Once the face is prepared for makeup, the makeup supplies are set out, and a brightly lighted location is decided upon, you are ready to apply the greasepaint.

APPLYING THE GREASEPAINT

The greasepaint can be applied to the face with brushes, sponges, fingertips, or the palms of your hands. The palms of your hands and the sponges are used to apply makeup to large areas of the face, such as white makeup on a whiteface clown.

Fingertips are used to apply makeup to smaller areas which require more control during application. Examples of fingertip application would be the areas around the eyes for an auguste or tramp clown, or the tramp's white mouth.

The brush is used in the smallest areas and to add lines to the face. Red mouths for both the whiteface and auguste are normally applied with a brush. Brushes are also used to apply makeup to eyebrows and the lines between colors.

When applying the greasepaint, start with the lightest color and progressively add darker colors. This is done because a dark color applied over the edge of a lighter color covers the lighter

color. However, the reverse is not true.

To reduce the chance of smearing the wet greasepaint, start the application of each color at the top of the face and work downward.

Frequently, after spending several minutes carefully applying makeup, you will develop an annoying itch. If you scratch it, you will ruin the makeup job you have been working on. What do you do? Rather than risk smearing your makeup, you may "scratch" your face by pressing the end of a toothpick against the spot that itches. If a toothpick is not available, use the end of the makeup brush opposite the bristles. This method is quite effective in eliminating the itch and works even after the makeup has been powdered.

Following the application of each color of greasepaint you must "pat out" the makeup. Pat each color, after it is applied, with the hands or fingertips. The purpose of the patting process is to take out the streaks in the greasepaint which were left when you first applied it to your face. When patted out properly, the colors on your face should have a nice smooth look with no streaks or thin spots.

As you pat out the makeup, be sure that the greasepaint is patted well in the creases and wrinkles on your face. If this is not done, excess makeup will remain in the creases, and it will not be absorbed or "dried" by the powder, which is applied in the next step. Thus, the makeup in the creases will move as you move your face. In a short period of time, the area with the excess makeup will have little or none left because the greasepaint will have migrated out of the crease, leaving an ugly line of bare skin showing.

CLOWN FACES WITH MUSTACHES AND BEARDS

Applying Makeup to a Mustache
Men who have mustaches can also become clowns. The mustache, however, creates some difficulty when designing the clown face and ap-

plying makeup.

Most tramp clowns leave the mustache natural (without applying makeup) and form the white mouth below the mustache. Since most mustaches reach the top of the upper lip on a person, the tramp clown will have a smaller mouth than he would without a mustache.

The whiteface and auguste clowns cover the mustache with clown white in their makeup scheme. Some apply the white makeup with their fingertips, but most use a toothbrush. Regardless of the method of application, the mustache should be recently shampooed. When the mustache has not been shampooed, the hair becomes coated with oil from the skin. These oils prevent the makeup from adhering well to the hair of the mustache.

Facial hair interferes with the design of the mouth causing problems for whiteface and auguste clowns. The stiff hair of the mustache limits the size and shape of the lips. Outlining with a black marker is also very difficult in the mustache area.

Having a mustache limits the lip designs you can use. The problems are not impossible to overcome, but you will have to spend a little more time than normal to finalize your design.

Applying Makeup to a Beard
Most clowns who have beards are tramp clowns. Whiteface and auguste makeup cannot adequately cover a beard. Some whiteface and auguste clowns choose to display their natural beards without makeup. In most cases this does not look good and should be avoided. Most tramp clowns display their natural beard without applying makeup. However, some tramp clowns will apply makeup to their natural beard. This is normally done with a toothbrush, similar to the method of applying makeup to the mustache. The beard, like the mustache, must be free of oil or the greasepaint may not adhere well.

The tramp who has a beard is limited to the size and shape of the white clown mouth he uses.

Normally the beard-free area around the lips is covered with clown white for the clown mouth. Only by shaving some of the beard around the mouth area can the size and shape of the clown mouth be changed.

If you have a strong desire to be a good-looking clown and are not too attached to your beard or mustache, consider shaving it.

POWDERING

Why Powder?
Powdering the makeup is absolutely essential for creating a professional looking clown face. When the makeup is applied to the face, it looks greasy and will smear unless it is "set" with powder. Talcum powder is normally used to apply the set. After the greasepaint has been powdered, it is dry to the touch and will not smear. Applying powder to the makeup also allows the skin to move while the greasepaint remains pliable and does not crack. This happens because the oil based greasepaint adheres to the skin, and the very fine talcum powder absorbs the oil from the makeup, thereby "drying" the greasepaint.

As the day wears on, sebaceous oils from the skin seep out of the pores and into the greasepaint-talcum powder. When more oils seep into the greasepaint-powder combination than the powder can absorb, the face becomes greasy. Repowdering will again set the greasy mixture and give a good dry appearance.

Many talcum powders are available on the market. They all work equally well. Powder can be applied to the face with either a sock or a powder puff.

The Sock Method
To use the sock method, fill a cotton (not a nylon) sock with powder, and tie the open end to prevent the powder from spilling out. Holding the top of the sock, shake the sock a few times to work powder through the fabric. Keep shak-

ing until a light coat of powder covers the exterior of the sock. Lightly pat the sock against the makeup on your face. Pat the white makeup first, going from the light colors to the dark colors.

When patting red or black colors, carefully pat the sock against your face, and hold it there for about two seconds, then remove it. When removing the sock, be careful not to smear the darker colors onto the lighter colors. Some colored greasepaint may be picked up by the sock from the face. This will not cause a problem, however, because the powder in the sock will dry the greasepaint.

After the sock has been removed from your face, turn it to the other side before making the next pat. If you do not turn the sock, some of the greasepaint picked up on the sock may not have had time to dry. This could result in smearing of darker greasepaint onto a lighter portion of your face.

Continue patting and holding the sock against your face until the surfaces of all the darker colors are powdered dry to the touch.

As soon as the entire face is lightly powdered, the surface of the greasepaint will temporarily feel dry. This means the powder can be applied heavily without fear of smearing the colors. Heavy powdering can be accomplished by patting hard and quickly over the entire face. *Be careful not to inhale the cloud of dust.* Some studies have indicated that there may be harmful effects from prolonged breathing of talc, so it is a good idea to keep this material out of your lungs.

A second way to apply powder is to tilt the head back and let the powder fall from the sock to the face. Daisy uses this method to apply powder. See Figure 6-14. Folding and unfolding the sock above the face allows the powder to escape from the sock and fall onto the face. After the face is covered reasonably well with powder, complete the powder application by patting the powder on the face with the sock.

Enough powder will coat the surface of the makeup that it will not transfer onto the sock.

Look in a mirror when you apply powder to make sure the powder job is heavy and complete. On the whiteface, however, a visual inspection may not be enough to tell if the face is entirely covered with powder. You will need to feel the entire face with the fingertips. Any area not completely covered with powder will feel greasy, sticky, or warm. These are called *hot spots* and must be repowdered.

The Powder Puff Method
Another method of applying powder is with a powder puff. An easy way to do this is to empty the talcum powder into a plastic margarine or Tupperware container. Place a standard powder puff into the powder. Then pat the puff against the face, transferring the powder from the puff to the face. The puff is stored in the container with the powder.

When using a puff, a cloud of powder dust is not raised, so it makes less of a mess. You can also see what you are doing better in the mirror. However, care must be taken with the puff so that the makeup is not smeared while applying the powder. Strutter uses a powder puff to apply powder to his makeup, see Figure 7-14.

Setting the Makeup
After the powder application, wait two to five minutes for the powder to absorb the oil from the greasepaint. You can tell when this happens because you will experience a tightening sensation on the surface of your face.

Removing Excess Powder
When the five or so minutes are up, remove the excess powder from the face. Powder can be removed with a paint brush, a makeup brush, a shaving brush, or a good sheepskin powder puff.

Most paint brushes have stiffer bristles and are less expensive than makeup and shaving brushes. More care must be used when removing excess powder with a paint brush because the stiffer bristles can smear one color onto another. Consequently, you should brush from the lighter color onto the darker color. Never brush from red to white. When brushing a black or red area, clean the dark tints picked up by the brush. The best way to do this is to vigorously brush the palm of the hand between strokes. This will clean the brush for the next stroke.

Powder Puff Method
One of the easiest ways to remove powder is to use a sheepskin powder puff. It does an excellent job without smearing the colors. Sheepskin puffs are available from clown supply dealers. They are well worth the expense.

Removing Powder Deposits
If, after brushing the powder, white powder deposits still adhere to the greasepaint, remove the deposits with a small foam sponge. These are sold at cosmetic counters and will do the job effectively.

After removing most of the dry powder with a brush or powder puff, you may find a slight amount still on the face. This may be removed by blotting the face with a damp sponge. Make sure that the sponge is just damp, not dripping wet. Just touch it to the face. Do not wipe the face. Wiping may smear the colors. This blotting will remove the excess powder and give a cool refreshing feeling to the face. It will also brighten the colors.

Water Set
Some clowns claim that it is necessary to use a damp sponge or a mist of water to set the makeup. This is not true. What this water does, other than remove the powder, is to harden the makeup by cooling it, caused by the evaporation of the moisture on the face. However, in about five minutes, the heat from the face will warm the makeup to the point it was before the water application, thus the set is lost.

Many clowns prefer to not use the water or sponge application to remove excess powder, even though the colors may not be as bright as they could be with the powder removed. Their reasoning is that in about 30 minutes, enough heat and oil from the face will have soaked up the excess powder, and the colors will be as bright as they would have been with the water application. This 30 minutes is just about the time it takes to get from the place of makeup application to the clown engagement.

Allergies
Some clowns have a mild allergy to orrisroot, the plant used to perfume baby powder. When clowning several consecutive days, they will develop a rash on their face. If you have a similar allergy, use non-scented talcs or sprays developed by makeup suppliers to set the greasepaint. The sprays do a good job, but they are expensive and leave a shiny appearance to the makeup.

Where to Apply Powder
Since powdering is messy, apply it outdoors if the weather permits. In cold or wet weather, it may be necessary to apply the powder in the home. If you have no garage or basement, apply the powder in the shower with the water off and the curtain pulled. This will prevent the powder from drifting all over the room, and it can then be washed down the drain next time you take a shower.

WET AND DRY METHODS

When applying clown makeup, one of two methods is used—the *wet method* or the *dry method*. Both methods start with the lighter colors and then progress to the darker colors. The major difference between the two methods is that in the dry method, powder is applied after the application of each color of makeup. In the wet method, all colors are applied before the makeup is powdered. There are advantages and disadvantages to each method.

The advantage of the dry method is that there are fewer chances for smears. The major disadvantage of the dry method is that once a mistake has been made, correction is extremely difficult without removing the entire makeup. Another disadvantage of the dry method is that you cannot blend one makeup into another.

Advantages of the wet method include being able to correct mistakes easily prior to powdering. A disadvantage of the wet method is the chance of smearing one color onto another while they are in the wet or unpowdered state.

Which method should you use? Only you can answer that question, after you have tried both methods and determined the one which works better for you.

AFTER POWDERING

The final steps in the makeup application are lining the face and attaching the nose. These processes are described in Chapters 11 and 10 respectively.

After you have become accustomed to applying a clown face, you will spend about an hour each time you do it. In the beginning you may need more time. Do not try to apply makeup too quickly or it will result in a sloppy job.

Step-by-step applications of the whiteface, auguste, and tramp faces are presented in the next three chapters. The wet method is used in the tramp demonstration. A combination of the wet and dry methods is used in the auguste demonstration, while the dry method is used in the whiteface demonstration.

Jack Anderson demonstrates his method of applying whiteface makeup in developing his clown character "Freckles." Delores Rademaker follows with her auguste makeup in the creation of "Daisy." The tramp clown is the author's character, "Strutter."

Chapter Five

Whiteface Makeup

Jack Anderson presents a step-by-step demonstration of how he brings his whiteface character, Freckles, to life. Figure 5-1 shows Jack cleanly shaven and ready to apply makeup. Jack begins by applying clown white with a sponge. See Figures 5-2 and 5-3.

The face is completely covered with clown white using the sponge and fingertips as shown in Figure 5-4.

The white makeup which has been applied, shows streaks from the application process. To remove these streaks and give the white an even, uniform appearance, Jack pats the entire area covered by makeup with his palms, fingers, or fingertips as shown in Figure 5-5. This gives a smooth matte finish to the makeup. Before beginning the powdering step, Jack removes the makeup from his hands with paper towels.

In Figure 5-6 Jack is shown with his head tilted back and working a powder filled sack like an accordion. This allows the powder to fall onto the wet makeup. Jack turns his head to each side to make sure that powder covers the entire face. After covering his face with a light coat of powder he gently pats the sock against the makeup to thicken the powder application (Figure 5-7). He next uses a sheepskin powder puff to pat the entire face, neck, and ears as shown in Figure 5-8. This step ensures that all of the clown white is thoroughly covered with powder.

After waiting 1-2 minutes Jack removes the excess powder with a shaving brush as shown in Figure 5-9. Jack next mists his face with water from a spray bottle as shown in Figure 5-10 to remove any excess powder from his face. Removing the excess powder is necessary in the dry application process. If excess powder is still on the face, other colors will be difficult to apply.

Following the face misting, Jack pats the face dry with a towel. It is necessary to pat

Figure 5-1

Figure 5-2

Figure 5-3

Figure 5-4

Figure 5-5

Figure 5-6

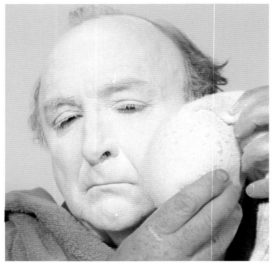

Figure 5-7

Figure 5-8

Figure 5-9

Figure 5-10

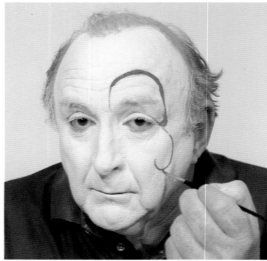

Figure 5-11

Figure 5-12

Figure 5-13

Figure 5-14

Figure 5-15

Figure 5-16

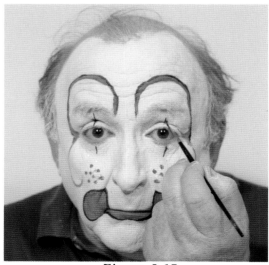

Figure 5-17

Figure 5-18

Figure 5-19

Figure 5-20

rather than wipe because the greasepaint could be smeared.

Jack's next step, after allowing the face to dry thoroughly, is to add his blue eyebrows. He does this with a ¹/₄ inch sable brush, applying Mehron's blue color cup makeup. Jack completes one side before moving to the other side as shown in Figure 5-11.

Jack's next step is to apply his mouth. His mouth consists of three parts: the bottom lip and two circles at the corners of his mouth. Figure 5-12 shows Jack forming the first circle.

You will notice that when a circle has been formed, it is filled with red greasepaint. Jack uses Mehron red, applying it with a ¹/₄ inch sable brush. Figure 5-13 shows Jack forming the lower lip of his mouth.

Jack applies his trademark, red freckles, in a unique way. He takes the end of the makeup brush opposite the bristles, touches it to the makeup, and then touches the end to his cheek. This method gives him freckles which are uniform in size and large enough to be seen from a distance (Figure 5-14).

Jack is now ready to begin the lining process. He uses Mehron black greasepaint from a color cup and applies it with a sable liner brush. Figure 5-15 shows Jack applying a black line on the top side of his blue eyebrow. This technique makes the blue stand out. In Figure 5-16, where Jack is starting to apply lines around the red of his mouth, you can see that the lining of the eyebrow does not carry down the blue curve which extends below the corner of the eye. Also, you can see that Jack applies lines only to the top of the eyebrow. This, he feels, allows the blue to stand out well enough without a black line below the blue eyebrow.

After Jack has outlined the red of his lips, he draws a vertical line down his eyelid (Figure 5-17). This line continues down below the eye.

At this point Jack's makeup application is complete. He is now ready to powder again as he did in Figures 5-7, 5-8, and 5-9. He also mists his face to remove excess powder and pats it dry as shown in Figure 5-10.

Once the face is completely dry, Jack is ready to put his clown nose into place. This nose

Figure 5-21

is held in place by monofilamant line attached to the nose. In Figure 5-18 he is shown with the nose in place. The line goes around the head above the ears.

Jack next puts on a skullcap made of white spandex (Figure 5-19). If you are not familiar with spandex, it is a stretchy material from which bathing suits are made. The skullcap is just a hood which goes over the head with an opening for the face. It covers the neck as well as the back of the head.

Whiteface clowns who do not use a hood or skullcap should cover their necks, front and back, and their ears with white makeup in order to prevent natural skin from beging visible.

With the addition of the wig (Figure 5-20) and wardrobe (Figure 5-21), Jack has completed his transition to Freckles. Notice how the face is balanced, the nose is sized to the other features of the face, and although open spaces are filled, the face is not cluttered.

Chapter Six

Auguste Makeup

Delores Rademaker demonstrates how she brings her auguste clown, Daisy, to life. Delores is shown in Figure 6-1 after her street makeup has been removed. A headband keeps the hair off her forehead. Delores's first step is to outline her eye mask area and mouth area with clown white using a $^3/_8$ inch sable brush. See Figure 6-2. Delores uses Kryolan white. In figure 6-3, Delores outlines her lips. She continues to fill in between the outlines with clown white applied with the $^3/_8$ inch brush as shown in Figure 6-4. You will notice that Delores does not cover her eyelids with makeup.

In Figure 6-5, Delores pats the white makeup to a smooth matte with her fingertips. Her patting actually smears the white makeup outside the original mouth lines she has drawn. She will correct this in the next step when she applies flesh makeup to the mouth and eye mask areas. Before applying the makeup, she takes a bit of flesh colored makeup from a Stein's velvet stick, places it in the palm of her hand, and kneads it with her fingertips. When the flesh colored makeup is warm, soft, and pliable, Delores applies it around the mouth and eye mask area with a $^3/_8$ inch brush, giving a clearly defined line between the white and flesh (Figure 6-6). Delores does not yet apply the flesh below her eyes. She does, however, cover the white which has been patted outside the original white outlines.

The next step for Delores is to fill in the areas of her forehead, around the eyes, and around the eye mask area with flesh colored makeup, applied with a $^3/_8$ inch brush as shown in Figure 6-7. This flesh makeup is then smoothed with her fingertips, as shown in Figure 6-8, and down onto the neck as in Figure 6-9.

Next, Delores takes Mehron red and mixes it with the flesh makeup in the palm of her hand. She applies this mixture around the mouth area

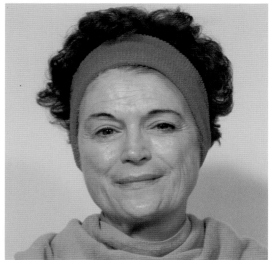

Figure 6-1

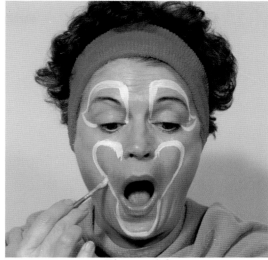

Figure 6-2

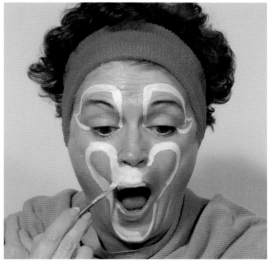

Figure 6-3

Figure 6-4

Figure 6-5

Figure 6-6

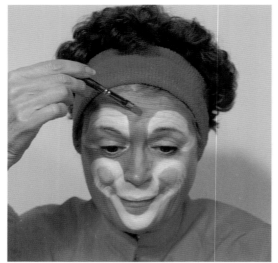

Figure 6-7

Figure 6-8

Figure 6-9

Figure 6-10

Figure 6-11

Figure 6-12

Figure 6-13

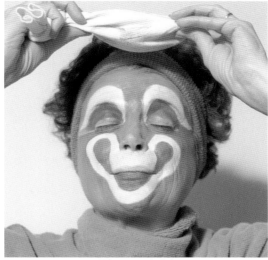

Figure 6-14

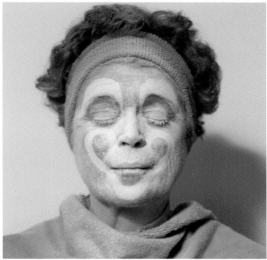

Figure 6-15

Figure 6-16

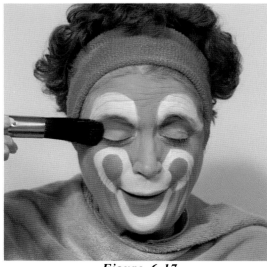

Figure 6-17

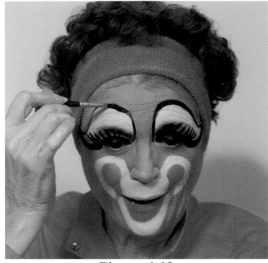

Figure 6-18

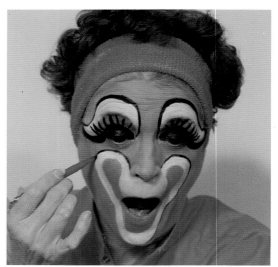

Figure 6-19

Figure 6-20

with a ³/₈ inch brush as shown in Figure 6-10. Delores then takes the remaining mixture of flesh and red makeup and applies a circular dot about the size of a dime on her forehead between the eye mask areas. She applies a small dot on each temple. These dots are applied with her finger tips. Delores then blends the red and flesh mixture with the base of flesh makeup using her fingertips. This gives her just the proper hue to the flesh colored makeup.

Next Delores powders the white makeup on her upper lip with a powder filled sock. She does this to keep the white from smearing onto the lower lip (Figure 6-11).

Mehron red is applied to the lip area with a ³/₁₆ inch brush as shown in Figure 6-12. Once makeup has been applied to the lower lip, Delores keeps her mouth opened slightly to prevent the red from smearing onto the white upper lip.

Mehron blue is applied to the area between the eyelid and the natural eyebrows with a clean ³/₈ inch brush. This mixes with the white makeup already applied to that area and gives the appearance of blue eyeshadow as in Figure 6-13.

Delores is ready to powder the makeup,

which she does with a powder filled sock. As shown in Figure 6-14, she tilts her head back and lets the powder fall onto the makeup by folding and unfolding the sock. Figure 6-15 shows the fully powdered face. Delores feels her face with her fingertips to be sure that the entire surface is well powdered as shown (Figure 6-16). If she finds a spot not completely covered, she applies powder to that area.

Unlike the whiteface of Jack Anderson described in the last chapter, Delores prefers not to mist her face with water, nor does she apply a damp cloth or sponge to remove excess powder. After waiting about four minutes for the powder to set the makeup, Delores removes the excess powder with a paint brush (Figure 6-17) and removes any powder residue with a shaving brush.

Delores uses Maybelline liquid eyeliner to cover the upper eyelid and to add eyelashes and eyebrows. She does this by pouring some of the eyeliner onto a small plastic tray, and applying it with a ³/₁₆ inch makeup brush. She first applies the liner to the eyelid and follows with the line between the eye mask area and cheek. Next,

Figure 6-21

Delores paints eyelashes, going from the natural eyelid to the natural eyebrow. Finally, Delores applies the liquid eyeliner above the mask area to form the eyebrow as shown in Figure 6-18. These eyes are Daisy's trademark.

The next step is to apply the black line around the mouth area and around the lips. Delores applies these lines with a Maybelline liner pencil as shown in Figure 6-19.

A ProKnows rubber nose is applied to the face with silicone adhesive. Once the application is completed, Delores blends the flesh colored portion of the false nose with that on the bridge of her natural nose as shown in Figure 6-20. This area is lightly powdered and then dusted with a shaving brush.

Following the addition of the wig, hat, and wardrobe, Delores has transformed herself into Daisy (Figure 6-21). Notice the balance of the face; the white around the mouth balances the white above the eyes, and with the addition of the nose the facial components are tied together.

Chapter Seven

Tramp Makeup

The author begins his character, Strutter, with a cleanly shaved face as shown in Figure 7-1. The first step is to outline the mouth and eye areas. This is done with a white Playbill pencil as shown in Figure 7-2. Kryolan white makeup is then applied with finger tips to the areas inside the white lines, beginning at the mouth and followed by the eye area (Figure 7-3). Although the white lines do not extend below the eyes, clown white is applied there. It will be blended with flesh colored makeup in a later step.

The next step is to apply the flesh colored greasepaint. Strutter uses Mehron's velvet stick. He applies this to all facial areas which have not been covered with white or the area of the nose that will be covered by a clown nose. This is done by dabbing the velvet stick directly onto the face as shown in Figure 7-4. The flesh colored makeup is then smoothed over the entire face (Figure 7-5). The reason for applying flesh in

the cheek area is that the red shows much brighter this way. On Strutter's face the red has an orange color when applied directly to the skin. However, if applied over the flesh makeup, the red shows up very brightly. Blending is also easier when the red is applied over the flesh color. Finally, the flesh makeup is used as a foundation in the beard area. When rubbed out, the black beard becomes a soft gray. If the black greasepaint is applied directly to the skin, a harsh black beard will result.

A gap of about $1/8$ inch is left between the flesh makeup and white makeup at the mouth and the white makeup above the eyes. Since the flesh and white makeup are blended below the eyes, care need not be taken in that area. The reason the gap is left is so that the black lines can be applied directly to the skin, which will be done in a later step. If the gap between the white and flesh needs to be widened to the $1/8$ inch dis-

Figure 7-1

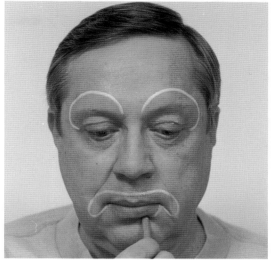

Figure 7-2

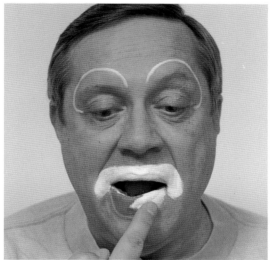

Figure 7-3

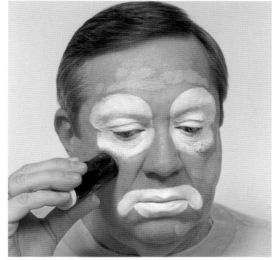

Figure 7-4

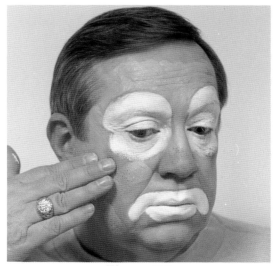

Figure 7-5

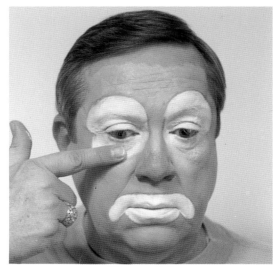

Figure 7-6

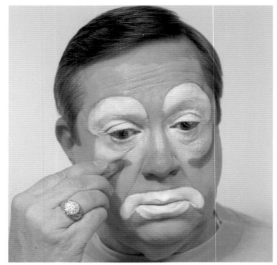

Figure 7-7

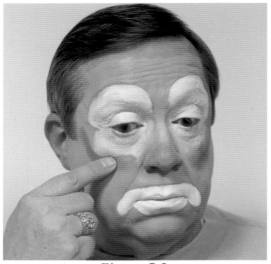

Figure 7-8

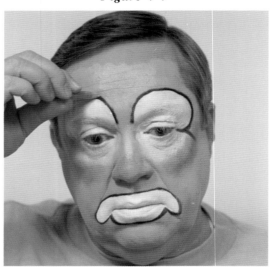

Figure 7-9

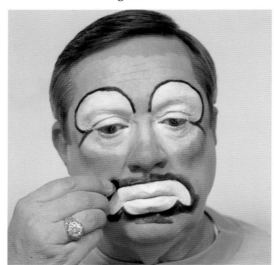

Figure 7-10

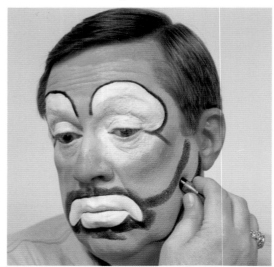

Figure 7-11

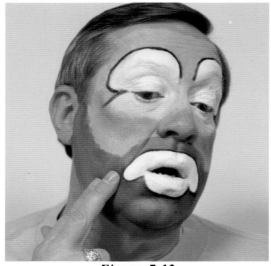

Figure 7-12

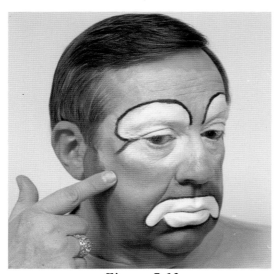

Figure 7-13

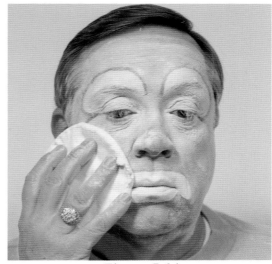

Figure 7-14

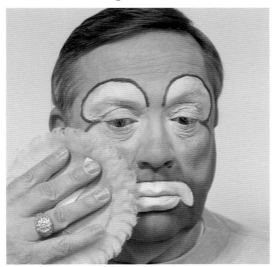

Figure 7-15

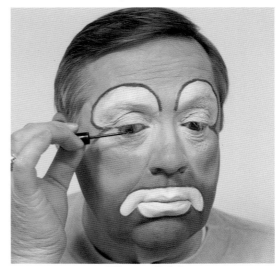

Figure 7-16

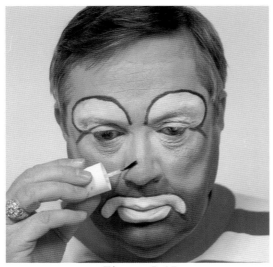

Figure 7-17

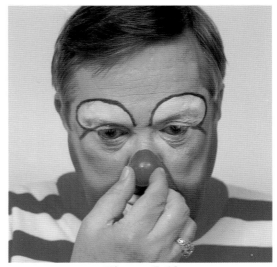

Figure 7-18

Figure 7-19

tance, trace over the area with a cotton swab.

Strutter takes flesh makeup on his finger and blends it with the white makeup below the eye (Figure 7-6). This darkens the area under the eye slightly, and it gives a nice blended transition from white to flesh.

Following the flesh color application a red liner stick is used to draw an arc under each eye along the cheekbone as shown in Figure 7-7. The red areas below the eyes are then blended down onto the flesh makeup of the cheeks and upward to blend with the white and flesh blend under the eyes (Figure 7-8).

After the application of the red makeup is completed, Strutter outlines his white mouth with a black Playbill pencil. He then outlines the white area above his eyes with the same pencil, starting at the inner eyebrow and finishing at the outer corner of the eye. He then draws crow's feet at the outer corner of each eye to help personalize his face and to highlight the *laugh lines*. (Laugh lines are the wrinkles which develop on the outside edges of the eyes when laughing or making a big smile.) The lines are drawn in the $1/8$ inch gap between the white and flesh colors. This keeps the lighter colored greasepaint from mixing with the black of the pencil. The result is a sharper and darker line (Figure 7-9).

To begin the beard application, makeup from a black liner stick is applied around the mouth area, as near to the black pencil line as possible (Figure 7-10). This is followed by applying a streak from the black liner stick along the top of the natural beard line. This streak runs from the bottom of the sideburns to the mustache area. This is followed by a streak from ear to ear running below the jawbone. A third line is drawn between these two in order to have enough makeup to cover the beard area (Figure 7-11).

The black makeup is then smoothed and blended with the finger starting with the area around the mouth, then moving to the sides of the face. After the black makeup has been smoothed and blended with the flesh-colored base, the beard takes on a nice gray tint. If a black beard is desired rather than the gray, the flesh-colored makeup is not applied to the beard area (Figure 7-12). The beard is then feathered

down onto the neck. At this point a harsh line remains at the edge of the beard line below the cheek as can be seen in Figure 7-12. This line is smoothed and feathered with the finger to softly blend the two colors (Figure 7-13). Notice the difference in the beard line in Figures 7-12 and 7-13. Many tramp clowns omit this last step, giving the beard a harsh look.

After making sure that all the makeup is smooth and patted, Strutter carefully powders by using a powder puff as shown in Figure 7-14.

Strutter powders well with the puff and waits 3-5 minutes for the powder to set. Excess powder is removed by dusting with a sheepskin powder puff as shown in Figure 7-15. The sheepskin puff removes the powder well enough that no other brushing is necessary.

Strutter now turns his attention to his eyes. He applies mascara to the upper lashes (Figure 7-16). This application of mascara covers any white makeup which has adhered to the eyelashes. As with any substance used near the eyes, a small amount should be used to test for allergic reactions before applying the full amount.

Strutter applies spirit gum adhesive to his nose and then sets the false nose in place (Figures 7-17, 7-18).

With the addition of a wig, hat, and wardrobe, Strutter's transition is complete (Figure 7-19).

Chapter Eight

The Clown Mouth

The mouth is the most important feature of the clown face and one of the most difficult to design. The first step in designing a clown mouth is to look at the bone structure of your face and the size of your natural mouth. Move the muscles. Look at how your face around your mouth moves. Choose a design that will move with your face. When you smile, your design should enhance the smile and make it bigger.

It is highly unlikely that the first mouth you try will suit you; if not, wipe it away and try another. Most clowns experiment with many mouth designs before they are satisfied.

For a neat whiteface clown, the design of the mouth is simple. Just cover the natural lips with red greasepaint as a woman would cover her lips with lipstick. However, the comedy whiteface and auguste mouths are more difficult to design. That is because their clown mouth is composed of three distinct parts. The first is the lower lip.

It can be as small as the natural lip or it can be much thicker extending down toward the chin. Although the lower lip may be thick, it should not extend beyond the corners of the natural mouth.

The second and third parts of the mouth are identical but on opposite sides of the mouth. I call these the *extensions* because they normally extend beyond the natural mouth.

Jack Anderson's character, Freckles, shown in Figure 5-21 has a mouth which consists of a lower lip the size of his natural lip and the two circular extensions extending beyond the corners of the mouth. Delores Rademaker's character, Daisy, in Figure 6-21 has a lower lip which is thicker than her natural lip and extends like inverted tear drops, giving a natural smile.

Look at the whiteface clowns in Figure 8-1 and auguste clowns in Figure 8-2. Pick out three parts of the mouth for each of these and decide

Figure 8-1 Whiteface clowns.

Terri Meister

Figure 8-2 Auguste clowns.

Terri Meister

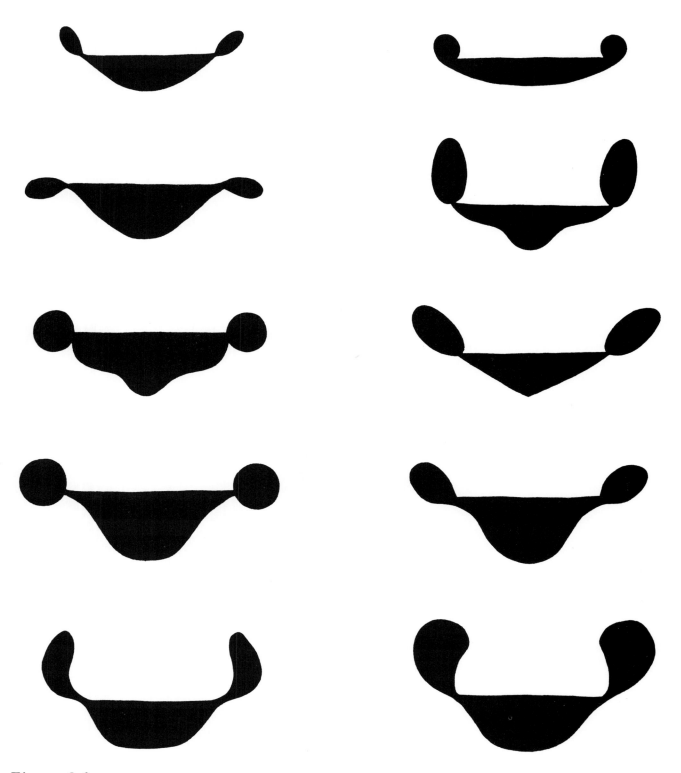

Figure 8-3

which ones look good and which ones don't look as good. Figure 8-3 shows sketches of a few mouth designs. Each consists of all three parts.

The tramp clown may have a mouth that is sad-shaped, happy shaped, or neutral depending on the character being portrayed. Figure 8-4 shows a group of tramp clowns with different shaped mouths. Figure 8-5 shows sketches of other tramp mouth designs.

GUIDELINES FOR THE CLOWN MOUTH

Some uninformed clowns surround their natural mouth in a large area of red makeup and think they have a great looking clown mouth. Nothing could be farther from the truth.

Since the mouth is the most expressive part of the face, the clown mouth should be sized and shaped to magnify the expression of the natural mouth. Therefore, there are several guidelines that should be followed when forming the mouth.

Neat Whiteface

The neat whiteface mouth covers only the lips of the natural mouth. Expanding the mouth size is a feature of a comedy whiteface and should be avoided if you are designing a neat whiteface.

The neat whiteface does not normally outline the lips in black. Because of the nature of the neat whiteface design, outlining is not done. Making the lips stand out does not fit with the simplistic design.

Auguste and Comedy Whiteface

The auguste mouth may be either red or black. The whiteface clown should use only red. With

Figure 8-4 Tramp clowns.   Terri Meister

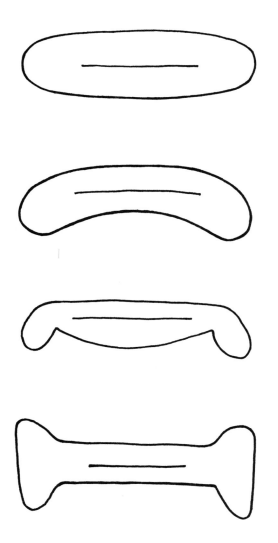

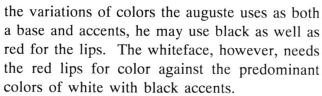

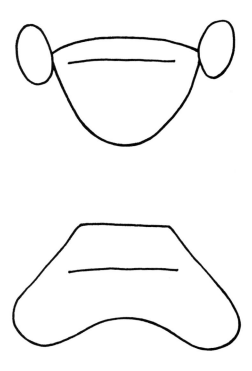

Figure 8-5

the variations of colors the auguste uses as both a base and accents, he may use black as well as red for the lips. The whiteface, however, needs the red lips for color against the predominant colors of white with black accents.

The auguste and comedy whiteface should not apply red or black to the upper lip. When red or black is applied to the upper lip and the mouth is opened, a hole shows up in the center of the red or black. However, with a white upper lip, a smile appears when the mouth is opened.

The outer edges of the mouth should not extend beyond a vertical line drawn through the outer edges of the eyes. All muscle control in the mouth area lies between these two lines. There is no control over the mouth outside this area. Therefore, expression is reduced when the mouth extends beyond the vertical lines (Figure 8-6).

Make sure the clown mouth is as wide as the natural mouth. Do not add a small heart or circle for the mouth. They do not enhance the natural mouth, cannot show the expressions that a clown needs to project, and adds nothing to the appearance to the clown face.

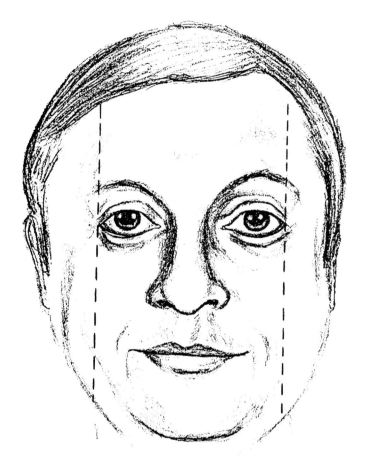

Figure 8-6

Tramp

The tramp clown does not use red, but may use black to extend the mouth line. By drawing a black line from the corners of the natural mouth, you can extend the mouth line. If these lines are drawn slightly downward, a sadder mouth is projected. Occasionally a tramp will color the lower lip black. This design is said to be more expressive than two white lips. Red lips do not fit the makeup scheme of a tramp clown.

The tramp mouth should not extend beyond the vertical lines drawn through the outer edges of the eyes. All muscle control in the mouth area lies between these two lines. Therefore, expression is reduced when the mouth extends beyond these vertical lines.

SMILE LINE

As a person ages, creases form in the skin beginning at the outer edges of the nose and running diagonally downward and outward to the outside of the mouth. These creases or lines are sometimes referred to as *smile lines*. They are the most used lines in the design of a clown face.

Figure 8-7

The sketch in Figure 8-7 show the smile lines.

Paul Glaros uses these lines to define the outer edge of his white makeup in the mouth area. Figure 8-8 shows Paul's character Chrissy with the smile lines as the outer edge of the white makeup.

Delores Rademaker uses the smile lines as the inner edge of Daisy's lips that extend above the natural mouth as shown in Figure 6-21. In Figure 7-19, the author uses the smile lines to define the outer edges of the white mouth for his tramp character Strutter, while Jack Anderson uses these lines to divide the circles which are extensions of Freckle's mouth. This can be seen in Figure 5-21.

When using the smile lines, you will probably notice that they are not symmetrical on either side of your face. Because of this problem it will be necessary to use one of these lines in the design of the clown face and draw the clown features on the other side of the face symmetrical to the first feature. This may result in you adjusting the smile lines on one side of the face.

WET METHOD LIP APPLICATION

If you use the wet method of makeup application, you cannot apply the red makeup for the lips on the top of the white makeup. Doing so

Figure 8-8

will give you pink lips. There are two ways to handle this problem. The first is to draw an outline of the lips and apply the white makeup around this outline, leaving the area uncoated where the lips will be applied. Delores Rademaker uses this method in Chapter 6.

The other way to handle the mouth problem is to completely cover the area with clown white and then wipe away the makeup from the area where the red makeup will be applied for the lips. This wiping away can be a accomplished by outlining the mouth design in the clown white with a toothpick. The white makeup within this outline is then wiped away with a tissue, paper towel, or cotton swab. The method you choose, or a combination of them, should be based on what works best for you. Once the white makeup has been "wiped out," the red makeup should be applied with a brush or cotton swab. Of course, care must be used to keep from smearing the red onto the white.

TEMPLATES

If you have trouble drawing your mouth or other features, you can use a template. Design your mouth on a piece of stiff cardboard and then cut the shapes out. Hold the template against your face and draw around it with a liner pencil. This takes away the guess work and allows you to have a nice uniform mouth or other feature.

Chapter Nine

Making Up the Eyes

The eyes, along with the mouth, are the most important parts of the clown face. Care should be given in making them stand out. A well designed clown face will have eyes that complement the mouth and will move with the muscles in the face to show action and expression.

EYE DESIGN

Makeup design of the eyes can be divided into three parts. The first is the *vertical line decoration* which is normally centered around the pupil. It is shown in Figure 9-1 as six semi-vertical lines above the eyeball. The second part of the eye design is the *outer edge decoration.* In the sketch it is shown as a mark extending from the outer edge of the eye in a downward direction. Finally, the third part of the eye design is the eyebrow.

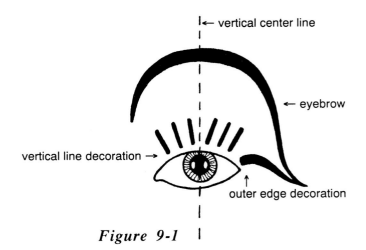

Figure 9-1

A properly designed clown eye does not necessarily need all three parts (vertical lines, outer decoration, and eyebrow). However, the eyebrow, being the most visible, is necessary in achieving a good eye design. The other two items are used to draw attention to the eye and convey emotions to the audience.

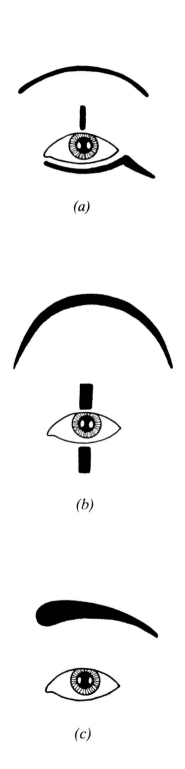

(a)

(b)

(c)

Figure 9-2

Figure 9-2a shows an eye with all these parts, while Figure 9-2b shows a well designed eye with only two components. Figure 9-2c shows the eye with only the eyebrow. All three of these eyes are well designed.

Several examples of each of the three eye components are shown in Figures 9-3 through 9-5.

Figure 9-3 shows twelve examples of vertical line decorations centered on the eye. These are above and/or below the eye, and in most cases are more than just lines. As you can see there are eyelashes, fan shaped markings, dots, and lines of various widths. All of them are centered on the vertical line running through the eyeball.

Figure 9-4 shows twelve examples of the outer eye decoration. These markings normally extend from the outer edge of the eye. Some, however, such as c and i, may also extend below the eye.

Figure 9-5 shows 18 examples of eyebrows. The first fifteen are for whiteface and auguste clowns while the last three are tramp clowns eyebrows. The eyebrows are varied in shape, size, and width of the lines.

Look at Figure 6-21, you will see that Daisy's eye design is a combination of 9-3j, 9-4j, and 9-5a. Strutter's eye design in Figure 7-19 is a combination of 9-4d and 9-5o.

By using the various combinations from Figure 9-3 through 9-5, you can develop over 3500 different eye designs. So use your imagination and the components shown here, or components of your own origin, to design your eyes. As you can see, it is not necessary to copy the exact eye design of another clown.

After deciding on your eye design, apply the eyes. See if they fit the shape of your face. If you are not perfectly satisfied with the results, try another design or modify the original.

When you have finally decided on your clown eye design, apply it to your face, along with your clown mouth. Check for balance and fit. If you

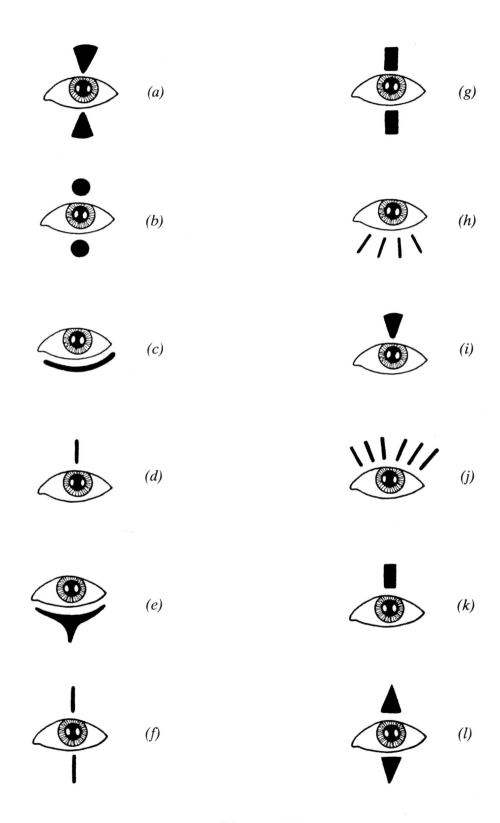

Figure 9-3

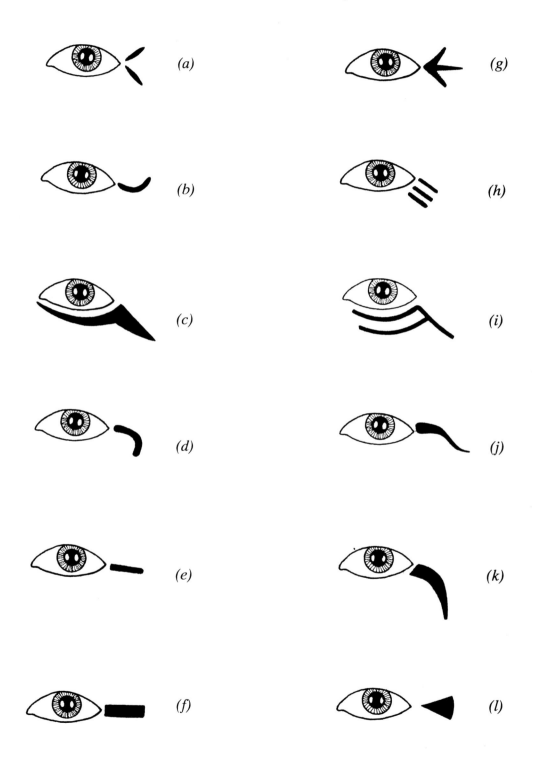

Figure 9-4

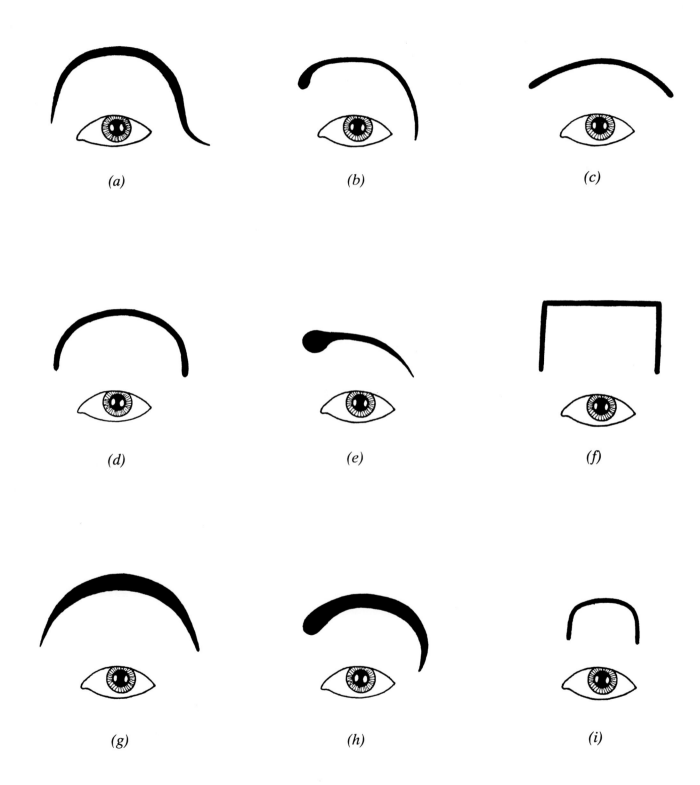

(a)   (b)   (c)

(d)   (e)   (f)

(g)   (h)   (i)

Figure 9-5

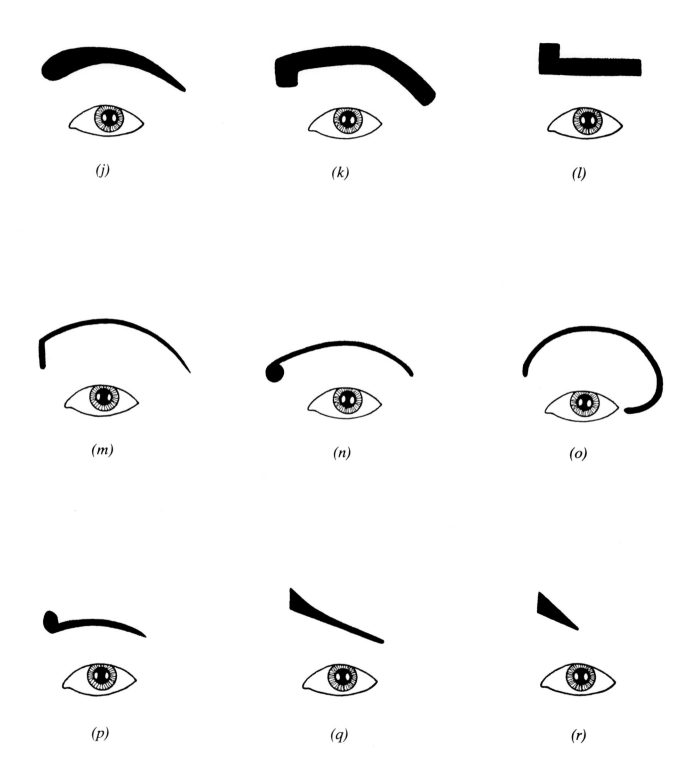

(j) (k) (l)

(m) (n) (o)

(p) (q) (r)

are not completely satisfied, modify either the eyes or the mouth until you have a well-balanced design which suits your character.

Eye makeup consists mainly of black lines. They are normally applied as you would apply lines to the other parts of the face. Lining techniques are given in Chapter 11.

THE INNER EYE

Three areas of the eye which are commonly overlooked are the lashes, the upper lid, and the area between the eye and the lash on the lower lid.

Eyelashes
Any clown white which gets onto the eyelashes should be removed. This can be done before powdering by wiping the lashes with a tissue. If you wait until after powdering, the makeup is almost impossible to remove. About the only thing left to do is cover the lashes with mascara.

False eyelashes are quite common on today's clowns. Some clowns use the regular cosmetic eyelashes while others go for the large clown lashes. The clown lashes are commercially available in two sizes, and which size is used is strictly a matter of taste. Chris "Sparkles" Warren is shown in Figure 9-6 wearing large eyelashes.

Clowns who wear glasses have found a way to use the false eyelashes. They glue them to the top of their glasses, and this fits in very well with the clown's character.

The Eyelid
Another step in highlighting the eyes is to add eye shadow to the upper lid. This can be done by applying commercial eye shadow to the eyelids after powdering. This eye shadow, which comes in a variety of colors, is in a dry form and can be purchased from any cosmetic counter.

Figure 9-6

Most eye shadow is sold with an applicator with which to apply it.

The eyelids can also be shaded by applying colored greasepaint to the lids on top of the clown white. It is then blended with the clown white to give the proper shade to the eye shadow. Daisy shades her eyes in this manner shown in Figure 6-13. Of course, this application takes place before powdering or lining the eyes.

Live Eye
The third highlighting technique is creating the *live eye*. This is nothing more than a dark line drawn on the lower lid between the inside of the lower lid and the lower lashes. The purpose of this line is to make the eye stand out by giving it more definition. However, caution should be used when applying this type makeup close to the eyeball. If you happen to be allergic to the marking pencil, you could develop a pair of sore eyes. To test if you are allergic to the makeup,

apply a small portion; if it causes irritation after a couple hours, discontinue using it.

You should also avoid using red, orange, and yellow makeup in or around the eyes. These colors contain chemicals that will cause eye irritation.

After applying powder to the face and removing the excess, take a liner pencil to apply the line on the thin portion of the lower lid between the eyeball and the lashes. This strip of skin is about $1/16$ of an inch wide.

When you are ready to apply the line, gently pull the lower lid away from the eyeball by placing the tip of your index finger on the center of the lower lid and pulling down. This moves the skin to be lined away from the eyeball and allows you to safely coat it with the liner pencil without contact with the eye. Pull the lower lid down only far enough to line it. Excessive pulling over a prolonged period of time could cause sagging of the lower lid.

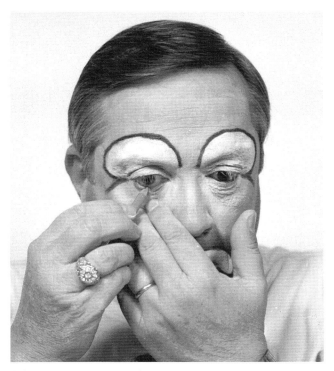

Figure 9-7

Once the lid is moved away from the eye, take the liner pencil and gently apply the black to the skin surface. Use several light strokes to apply the live eye rather than one or two heavy ones. You will be amazed at how easy it is to apply the live eye in this manner. Strutter demonstrates the application of the live eye in Figure 9-7.

Once the eye lid is released, the line is in place and the overall appearance of the eye is greatly improved.

EYEGLASSES

Most clowns do not wear glasses while clowning because it is very difficult to work a pair of glasses into a makeup and costume scheme. Some people, however, cannot see well enough to function without corrective lenses. Many clowns solve this problem by wearing contact lenses. But those who can't wear contact lenses must wear glasses.

If glasses are to be worn with the clown makeup, they must complement the wearer's clown face and costume. What alternatives are available to make their glasses fit their clown character? Some clowns wear wire rimmed glasses, other clowns take wire framed reading glasses—those half glasses which many middle aged people use when they read—and fit them with their corrected lenses. One of the best types of glasses to use are rimless glasses. Rimless glasses are good because they are not very noticeable and tend to blend in with the overall makeup scheme.

For those clowns who can afford custom glasses, heart shaped and star shaped glasses are available. Pat "Posty" Frank is shown with her prescription heart shaped glasses in Figure 9-8.

Others find comedy frames and have their prescription lenses placed in them. Sherry "Rainbow" Fast's unique glasses spell "LOOK"

Figure 9-8

Figure 9-9

Figure 9-10

with the lenses in the two O's (Figure 9-9).

Some unusual frames can work well if the color and style match your costume and makeup. Glasses can also be painted or decorated to fit your clown character. Figure 9-10 shows Happi and Mrs. Krako with their glasses.

Frank "Fashoo" Wisniewski has taken a pair of brightly decorated sunglasses and replaced the dark lenses with his prescription lenses. In Figure 9-11 you can see Fashoo with his unique glasses.

If you do wear glasses while clowning, do not wear the glasses you usually wear. In most cases they will not fit into the scheme of your clown character. Wear something special. Also, do not wear the photo sensitive lenses which darken in the sunlight. Nothing looks worse than a clown in sunglasses.

Figure 9-11

Chapter Ten

Clown Noses

All clowns must have a clown nose, whether it is simply a little paint on the natural nose or a bulbus false one. This chapter deals with different types of clown noses and techniques for forming and applying a custom-designed putty nose.

PAINTED NOSES

The simplest of noses is the painted nose. This is done by just painting the natural nose with red greasepaint. Painted noses are suitable for the whiteface clown, but the auguste and tramp look best with false noses.

Painted noses can be as small as a round circle on the end of the natural nose or as large as the entire nose. Normally something between these two extremes is most suitable. Noses can be dressed up by adding glitter. Sparkles is shown in Figure 9-6 with a painted nose.

FALSE NOSES

False noses can be custom made from latex or foam, formed from putty, purchased commercially, or constructed from an object such as a ball.

Many commercial clown noses are available, but the three most popular are the latex noses, which adhere to the natural nose; the clip-on noses, which are squeezed open and held onto the natural nose by friction; and round foam noses, which are also attached by adhesive.

Latex Noses
The latex noses are thin, lightweight, and generally comfortable. They are manufactured by many companies. One problem in the past with latex noses was the method of adhering them to the natural nose. When latex adhesive was used, latex would build up on the false nose and even-

Figure 10-1 The ProKnows combines characteristics of both the foam and latex noses. Light-weight, form fitting, and easily applied with adhesive they come in a variety of shapes and sizes.

tually the nose had to be discarded. Spirit gum was the alternative, but it would sensitize some skins and was somewhat difficult to remove. When either of these adhesives is used, the adhesive has to be reapplied each time the nose is attached to the face.

However, silicone adhesive allows the removal and replacement of the nose without reapplying the adhesive. This is particularly handy in cold weather when moisture from breathing condenses inside the nose or if the nose is running and needs to be wiped frequently. Boho wears a latex nose as shown in Figure 1-4.

Clip-On Noses
The clip-on noses are either vinyl or rubber. When the nose is squeezed, it opens and can easily be placed over the natural nose. When the pressure is released, the false nose closes onto the natural nose. Friction holds it in place. The advantage of this nose is that it is easily removed and replaced. The disadvantage is that the nose will not fit all clowns. Because of the shape of

some people's natural noses, clip-on noses sometimes do not hold well and fall off. For others, these false clip-on noses will close their nostrils, forcing them to breathe through their mouths. Muggs makes use of the clip-on nose as shown in Figure 3-2.

Vinyl Noses
Round vinyl noses held in place by string or monofilament lines are commercially available. The advantage of this type of nose is that adhesive is not required and the nose may be removed temporarily if needed. Of course, if the monofilament line breaks, you are out of luck. Freckles is shown wearing the nose in Figure 5-21.

Foam Noses
Round foam rubber noses are commercially available. They are merely foam balls with a slit cut in them. Before they can be used, foam from the interior of the ball must be removed. Otherwise, the foam nose would not fit well onto the clown's natural nose. This excess foam is best

removed with a pair of scissors.

It is less expensive to make your own foam nose out of round foam balls rather than buying a foam nose. With foam balls, which are available in many sizes, a properly sized nose can be worn on the face. The foam nose is attached with adhesive. Paul "Chrissy" Glaros is wearing a foam nose in Figure 8-8.

PUTTY NOSES

Although the putty nose is seldom seen outside the ranks of circus clowns, it is a great nose for any clown to utilize. It can be formed into just about any shape the clown would desire. Makeup can be applied to the nose so colors can easily blend into the makeup on the face.

Nose putty, also known as *nose and scar wax*, is commercially available from several manufacturers. Most stores which sell theatrical makeup will also have nose putty. The putty is available in tins or it may be wrapped in waxed paper and packaged in a cardboard tube.

To prepare your natural nose for the nose putty, make sure it is clean and free from oil or perspiration. If you have prepared your face for makeup, your natural nose is ready for the putty. The putty nose is applied before putting makeup on the face.

To prepare the putty, remove the amount needed and knead it with your fingers and thumb until it is soft and pliable. One word of caution: Keep your fingers damp with water. Once the putty has been handled, it becomes tacky like bubblegum. It will, therefore, stick to any surface that is not coated with water. So, it is necessary to keep your fingers damp when handling the putty.

Once the putty has been kneaded to a smooth pliable state, roll the putty into a round ball between the palms of your hands. Again, make sure your palms are damp. Next, make an indentation into the ball with your thumb. This indentation should be $3/8$ inch to $1/2$ inch deep so that your natural nose will fit into it. Since the indentation will be damp, the putty will not readily adhere to your natural nose. In order to dry the surface of the putty, blow into it. Then press the putty firmly onto your nose. See Figure 10-2.

After the putty has been applied, smooth and feather the edges on to your natural nose. See Figure 10-3. This will take a bit of work. By the time the edges are finished, the putty will be adhering to your natural nose. Now is the time to form the final shape of the nose. This can be done by smoothing and shaping with your fingertips. It is still necessary to coat the fingertips with water in order to smooth the putty. Some clowns simply lick their fingertips with their tongue. You may wish to use a more sanitary method.

The putty nose should fit onto the tip of your natural nose, leaving the nostrils open for breathing. If you attempt to cover the entire nose, you will encounter several problems. First, it is very difficult to form the putty around the nostrils. Second, if the putty covers the side of the nose and touches the cheek, a crack will form in the putty when you smile. Third, if you cover the bridge of the nose, you will end up with a very large, heavy nose.

In extreme heat, the putty may begin to droop after a few hours. If this happens, just go to a mirror and reshape the nose to this original contour. Makeup repair may also be required.

The nose putty can be colored with standard makeup. It is applied to the putty in the same manner as it is applied to the skin of the face. In figure 10-4 the author is applying makeup to the nose with a red liner stick. Once applied, the red is then smoothed over the nose with the fingertip.

It is not uncommon for a putty nose to receive nicks or scratches while it is being worn, creating a gap in the makeup. The putty color

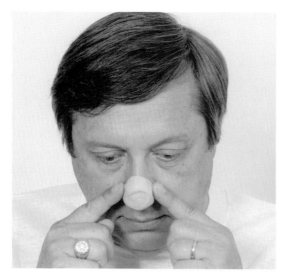

Figure 10-2

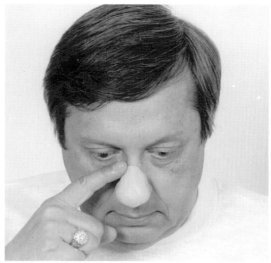

Figure 10-3

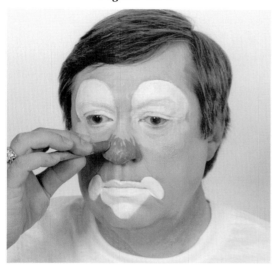

Figure 10-4

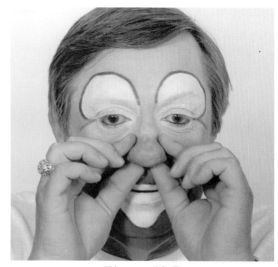

Figure 10-5

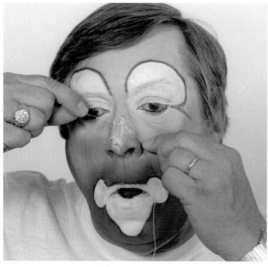

Figure 10-6

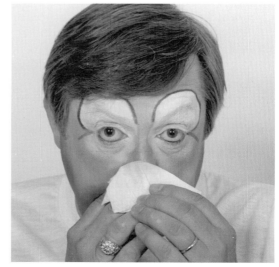

Figure 10-7

will show. It is, therefore, necessary to smooth out the nicks and touch up the color with makeup. Care should be used when drinking from a glass as the rim can nick the nose very easily.

To remove the putty nose, start peeling back the edges, beginning at the bottom. Continue this action, rolling the edges toward the center. See Figure 10-5. The fingers should be damp during this step. After the bulk of the putty has been removed, take a piece of cotton thread about 18 inches long. Pull it along your nose where the remaining putty adheres. The thread will separate the putty from your nose as is shown in Figure 10-6. Finally, remove any putty residue with spirit gum remover as shown in Figure 10-7.

A good way to store the putty between uses is to roll it into a ball and wrap it in a cloth saturated with baby oil. Place the wrapped putty into a plastic zip lock bag. It can be stored without damage and be ready for the next use.

Putty noses have several advantages over other artificial noses. First, they can be sized and shaped according to your taste. Second, no condensation will form inside the nose in cold weather. Third, they leave the natural nostrils exposed so that you can wipe your nose if it runs; and fourth, no adhesive or strings are required to attach the false nose to your face.

Putty noses also have disadvantages. First, they are heavier than other false noses. Second, it takes more time to apply and remove them, and third, they are easily nicked or damaged and require reshaping.

Putty noses are applied prior to the makeup, while the other false noses are added after the makeup and powder application.

When deciding on a nose, pick one that fits your character and the symmetry of your face and, by all means, choose one that is comfortable.

Chapter Eleven

Applying the Liner

PURPOSE OF LINING

Lining on the clown face serves three purposes. The first is to help provide a contrast between adjoining colors on the face. An example would be the line around the white mouth area of the auguste clown. The second purpose of lining is to apply decorations to the face, such as eyebrows or eyelashes on the auguste or whiteface clown, or crow's feet on the tramp. The third and most important purpose of the lining is to cover the areas of overlap where two colors on the face meet. It is very difficult to keep the line between the white and flesh colors on an auguste face uniform. One line will almost always smudge onto the other slightly, or they will not completely meet. The black lines cover these mistakes. Of course, when two colors are blended together, such as the red cheek area and the flesh colors on an auguste, no lining is required. Lines can be applied in any of three ways: with liquid eyeliners, eyeliner pencils such as Maybelline or Playbill, or with greasepaint applied with a brush.

Drawing black lines on the face is one of the most difficult parts of putting on a clown face because liquid liner easily smears or smudges. Long, smooth, flowing strokes are difficult to achieve with a brush. Many times a series of short strokes are used instead. This gives an irregular line. A china marker or eyeliner pencil does not give as dark a line although it is easier to control than the liquid. Greasepaint applied with a brush is slow and in many cases hard to set with powder. So, there is no easy way to apply lines to a clown face.

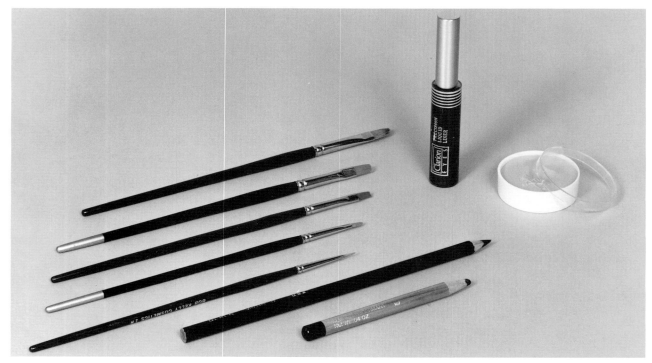

Figure 11-1 Liquid liner, greasepaint, liner pencils, and brushes.

LIQUID LINER

Liquid liner is the most commonly used liner. It must be applied after powdering or the powder will produce a dull effect. Be careful because the final removal of powder with a damp sponge may cause the liner to run. The liquid liner is packaged with a brush which is used in its application. When applying the liquid liner, use the following rules:

• Rest the elbow of the hand drawing the line on a solid surface such as a table top. An arm moving about is almost impossible to control.

• Brace the wrist of the hand drawing the lines by holding it with your other hand. This offers a stationary hand and permits lining to be controlled by the fingers.

• Hold your breath while drawing the line. Just a simple motion, like breathing, will cause irregularities in the lines.

• When possible, hold your hand and brush still, and move your face. It is much easier to move the face than the hand. Try it, you will be surprised how effective it is.

• Use long, smooth, flowing motions to draw the lines. Too many people are afraid that they will mess up by doing this, and they use short, choppy strokes, which, too often, shows in the finished line.

• Keep the bristles of the brush parallel to the lines being drawn. It may be necessary to get your hand in an awkward position to do this. If you do not, you will have lines of varying widths producing unsatisfactory results.

LINER PENCILS

The pencils used in lining are of two types. The first is a china marker, which is somewhat hard, and the second is a liner pencil, such as ones sold by Maybelline or Playbill.

Lines applied with the china marker are normally applied after powdering because the material will not smear. However, lines made with the softer pencils should be powdered or they may smear.

The same rules listed above in applying lines with the liquid liner apply to those made with the pencil except the last one, which has to do with keeping the brush parallel to the line. Lines from pencils are not as bright as those from a liquid liner, but some clowns are willing to make a compromise for the ease and quickness of application.

GREASEPAINT

The third method of lining is to apply greasepaint with a $1/4$ inch sable or hobby brush. The disadvantage of this method is that the lines are normally wide and the greasepaint is thick. This requires some very intense powdering in order to dry the thick greasepaint. The lines are brighter than those formed with a pencil but in some cases a bit duller than the lines drawn with liquid. Experiment to pick the type of lines that suit you best.

MISTAKES

What do you do when you make a mistake while lining your face? If you make a spot too wide, just widen the entire line. There is, however, a limit as to how far you can go. If the line matches an identical line on the other side of your face, you must also widen it. A last resort on mistakes is to take the lines off completely and start again.

When lining around the eyes, especially if the skin is loose, it may be necessary to draw the line toward the eye rather than away from it. This is particularly true when drawing a line down from the lower lid. If your skin is loose, draw upward toward the eye.

If the lines are wet above the eye, use care when putting on your wig. It is easy to drag the front of the wig through these upper lines and smear them to the point that they must be replaced.

Chapter Twelve

Makeup Problems and Repair

MAKEUP PROBLEMS

Every person who applies makeup occasionally encounters problems with the final result, usually due to a miscue in the application such as a crooked line or a smear. However, other problems, whose cause may not be apparent, may also be encountered. Among them are flaking, streaking, greasiness, splotches, and dull colors.

Flaking
When makeup flakes off the skin, either the skin was wet when the makeup was applied, or the makeup was applied too thickly. This problem affects the whiteface clown in the neck area more than any other place. The only way to solve the problem is to remove the makeup, dry the skin, and start over, making sure that the application is not too thick.

Talcum powders containing cornstarch will also cause flaking.

Streaking
Streaking shows up when the makeup is not completely patted out or smoothed. Different brands of makeup react to individual skins differently. What works for you may not work for another clown. However, most streaking problems are the result of not patting the makeup properly before powdering. Waiting to pat until after the powdering application will result in streaks. Not cleaning the excess oils from the face prior to makeup application will also make the makeup harder to pat out and can contribute to steaking.

Greasiness
Greasiness is the result of improper powdering. Care at the time of the powder application will, in most cases, prevent this problem. However, if the oils have not been washed from the face prior

to makeup application, the properly powdered face can quickly become greasy again. An additional application of powder will solve this problem.

Splotches
Splotches are not uncommon in warm weather areas in the summer months. Splotches are irregular white spots where the clown white is uneven. This is caused by perspiring while applying the makeup. If the weather is hot and air conditioning or a fan is not available, splotching will occur. Some clowns stand in front of an open refrigerator while applying makeup to prevent splotches. If splotches show up on your clown face, take the makeup off, dry the face, find a cooler place, and reapply the makeup. Splotches can also result from applying a sponge, which is too wet, to the face.

Dull Colors
Dull colors can result from two conditions. If ladies do not remove their everyday makeup before applying clown makeup, the two mix and produce a dull or beige tint to the clown white and a somewhat orange shade to the red. Of course, the solution to this problem is to remove cosmetic makeup before applying clown makeup. The only way to solve the problem after the fact is to remove the makeup and start over.

Dull colors can also result from the pigment in a person's skin. Clowns with ruddy faces or reddish skin tones normally have no problems with the red makeup since it shows bright and vibrant on their skin. However, those who have a great deal of yellow pigment or are heavily suntanned may find problems with poor coverage of their skin with white, and sometimes with the reds developing an orange cast. In order to make the area brighter, some clowns resort to liquid makeup or dry rouges. Strutter applies his red over a flesh colored base in order to produce a bright red. See Figures 7-7 and 7-8.

MAKEUP REPAIR

Many variables determine how long a makeup job will last before needing repair or replacement. Among the things to consider are: how oily your complexion is, what kind of makeup you use, the temperature where you will be working, how well you powder, how heavily you perspire, and what the condition of your facial skin is. Regardless of these conditions, sooner or later your makeup will need attention.

The first area to show signs of deterioration is usually around the lips. This problem can be followed quickly by creases or folds in the skin, areas rubbed by clothing, and miscellaneous smears.

Makeup repair can be divided into three categories: 1) Touch-up, 2) Repowder, and 3) Major Repair. The touch-up would include repairing a smear or light addition of makeup to the lips. The repowder, as the name implies, is the addition of more powder to combat greasiness, while a major repair would include both touch-up and repowder, as well as repairing other areas of makeup deterioration.

Touch-Up
The touch-up can be done in any out of the way place such as a restroom or car. If a small spot needs to be repaired, repowdering may not be necessary. Liner sticks are ideal for repairing the mouth. When touching-up the mouth, repowdering is definitely recommended. Powder several times lightly rather than one heavy powder in order to not dull the black lines on the face.

Repowder
When your face becomes greasy looking, it is time to repowder. This will restablize the makeup and prevent smears or further deterioration. Repowder in the same manner which you originally powdered. Ideally, find an out-of-the-way place where you can remove your wig and cover your costume.

After powdering, it may be necessary to re-draw your black lines. This will depend on what type liner you use and how bright you want the lines to appear.

Major Repair

When it is necessary to do a major makeup repair, you need to have most of your makeup with you and find a place where you can work without interruption. Ideally, it should be cool so that perspiration will not cause splotches on the areas of makeup reapplication. One way to cool your face is to mist it with a spray bottle of water and let it dry prior to the repair.

After cooling yourself off and removing your wig, repair the makeup by going from the light-est color to the darkest. Additional makeup can be applied over existing makeup with fingers, brushes, and cotton swabs.

Lines from some liquid eye liners have a ten-dency to flake. If this happens, use a small spatula or tweezers to remove the flaking liner before reapplying.

Complete the repair by powdering thorough-ly, just like the powdering when you originally applied your makeup.

After you remove excess powder, do not blott the face with a damp sponge or mist the face with water. Doing so may cause the liner to streak.

If the makeup is in extremely poor condition you may choose to remove the old makeup and apply it again from scratch.

Chapter Thirteen

Makeup Removal and Care

REMOVING MAKEUP

Baby Oil

There are as many methods for removing make-up as there are for applying it. One accepted method for removing the makeup is to use baby oil. To do this, saturate cotton balls or several folds of toilet tissue with the baby oil. Then, starting at the top of your face, rub the oil onto the makeup. Leave the eye sockets for last.

After rubbing the oil onto the face and giving it time to soak into the makeup, use cotton balls, paper towels, a few folds of toilet tissue, or a wash cloth to remove the softened makeup. It may be necessary to do this two or three times before the makeup is completely removed.

To remove makeup from the eye sockets, saturate a cotton ball with the baby oil and rub onto the remaining makeup. It will be almost impossible to keep the baby oil and some make-up out of your eyes. When this happens, your eyes will blur for a few seconds, but the blurring will not cause any harm.

After your eyes clear, use a dry cotton ball and wipe away the softened greasepaint. A second application may be necessary to remove all the makeup in the eye socket area.

You may notice in a few minutes that a small amount of white makeup has collected at the inside corners of your eyes. If you pull your lower eyelid away from the eyeball, you may notice a white string of makeup inside your lower eyelid. This can be easily removed by carefully touching it with your finger and slowly sliding it outside. The makeup in the corner of the eye can be removed in a similar fashion.

A second method some clowns use to remove makeup is to stand in the shower and pour baby oil into the cupped palm of their hands and thoroughly rub it all over their faces. They use enough baby oil to completely soften the grease-paint and then proceed to take their shower. This method sometimes leaves a little bit of white makeup near the eyelashes on the eyelids.

Allergies

Some people are allergic to baby oil. If that is the case, cooking oil can be substituted for the baby oil. It is just as effective, is non-toxic, and can be swallowed with no adverse effect. If you are allergic to baby oil, do not use mineral oil to remove the makeup since baby oil is mostly mineral oil.

If you use a cloth such as a towel or wash cloth to remove the makeup, don't worry about the stain. It will wash right out.

Liquid Soap

If you do not want to go through the mess of makeup removal with oil, try liquid soap. Many clowns use liquid soap, dishwashing detergent, liquid hand soap, or hair shampoo to remove the makeup.

The soaps should be kept away from the eyes. Even the neutral shampoos which do not burn the eyes can cause some discomfort.

Many other items will remove makeup, including cold cream, petroleum jelly, hair tonic, and alcohol. Even spirit gum remover will soften the makeup. Cold cream and petroleum jelly are effective around the eyes. The others, however, will irritate the eyes severely and should be not be used in these areas.

Baby Shampoo

The author uses Johnson's Baby Shampoo to remove the makeup from his face. He applies it to makeup and thoroughly rubs the shampoo into the makeup with his fingertips. He purposely avoids the eye socket area. He then uses a wash cloth to remove the makeup softened by the shampoo. After the face has been rinsed, he applies cold cream to the makeup at the eye socket with his fingertips. He then removes the residue with a cotton ball.

Skin Care

Some clowns who wear makeup on a regular basis develop mild rashes or skin irritations on their face. Vitamin E, which soothes and heals the surface of the skin, can help overcome these rashes and irritations. Vitamin E in liquid form can be purchased from your local drug store.

CARING FOR YOUR MAKEUP

In order to keep your makeup and supplies in good condition, you should have a makeup kit exclusively for your makeup and supplies. Small fishing tackle boxes, train cases, and sewing cases are some items clowns use for makeup kits.

When you are applying your powder, make sure that the lids on your makeup containers are shut. Powder falling onto the makeup will have a tendency to dry it out.

Brushes

After each makeup application, clean your makeup brushes. They can be cleaned by first wiping any excess greasepaint from them with tissue paper. Then remove the balance of the greasepaint with baby oil or liquid soap. The brushes should be dry before putting them away.

Brush cleaners are also available which makes cleanup almost effortless.

Effects of Heat

Excessive heat is the greatest enemy of clown makeup. Leaving your makeup in a closed car exposed to the summer sun can effectively ruin it. The heat will cause the liner sticks to melt, and when they resolidify, they are misshapen and must be discarded. The same is true for the velvet sticks. Liner pencils will harden, and the lines drawn with them will not be dark or true. They also should be discarded. Makeup in cups will lose the uniform consistency they normally have. Sometimes the color will dull when exposed to excess heat.

Keeping the Makeup Cool
The best way to avoid excess heat is to keep makeup at home out of the heat. Sometimes, however, it is necessary to keep your makeup nearby. Delores Rademaker has a technique she uses to keep her makeup from melting in the summer heat.

She purchased an insulated canvas bag at a local discount store. Sized to hold a six-pack of canned drinks, it measures about 6"x6"x9". She uses this bag as her makeup kit in the summertime. However, if she is going to be out for any length of time, she puts blue ice, a blue liquid encased in plastic, in the bag. When frozen, blue ice functions like ice and will keep the makeup cool.

Delores wraps the blue ice in a towel and places it in the bottom of the insulated bag. Although the blue ice is sealed and will not leak, wrapping it in towels keeps moisture from condensation away from the makeup.

Chapter Fourteen

Clown Wigs

Many clowns take great pains to apply their makeup properly and spend a great deal of money on their wardrobe then spoil their appearance by wearing a wig which does not suit their character. Suitable wigs must be the right size, the right color, properly trimmed, and groomed.

The costume should be chosen before picking the wig so it will fit into the overall scheme of the makeup and costume.

The wig should not be the same color as the color immediately below your chin. If it is, the face will seem to be detached and floating, totally surrounded by that color.

Try on different colored wigs while you have your makeup on. You will be surprised how differently you look by simply changing the color of your wig.

Clown wigs are not graded by size, so a wig should always be tried on before purchasing. An uncomfortable wig can be pure torture after several hours in makeup so finding the proper size should be a major concern when you select a wig.

WIG TYPES

Many types and colors of clown wigs are commercially available. Wigs come in various styles including curly, straight, bald, or afro and are available in many colors, including multicolor. Wigs are made from natural hair, synthetic hair, and yak hair, as well as from yarn and fake fur.

The *afro-style wig* is the most commonly used. Mama Clown, shown in Figure 1-2, is wearing an afro wig. Afro wigs are constructed of very tightly curled nylon "hair" attached to a mesh cap. These wigs require a great deal of attention before they can be worn. The hair on these, as well as most other wigs, is too long and must be trimmed. The afro must be combed or picked with a pick comb before trimming. Check where you purchase your wig, since many of the dealers will pick and trim your new wig for a small fee.

Curly wigs are similar in construction to the afro wigs, except the curls are much looser. Chris Warren's character, Sparkles, shown in Figure 9-6, is wearing a curly wig. Curly wigs need to be combed out and trimmed in a manner similar to the afro. However, the curly wig will require less time to prepare than the afro. Long curly wigs are becoming popular with clowns who portray a female character.

Straight wigs, sometimes called the *silly boy* style, are also constructed from nylon hair attached to a mesh cap. Strutter is wearing a silly boy wig in Figure 7-19. These wigs must also be trimmed before wearing.

Yak wigs are the best quality and appear fuller and thicker than synthetic hair. They are, as the name implies, made from the hair of the

yak, or a wild ox. Yak wigs are much bigger than those made from synthetic fibers. They cost five to ten times as much as synthetic wigs. Jim "Dune Buggy" Russell, shown in Figure 14-1, is wearing a straight yak wig.

Yak wigs are available in a variety of colors, curly or straight, full head or bald pate (the crown of the head being bald with hair on the sides). Yak wigs, which run larger in size than synthetic wigs, must also be trimmed and shaped like other wigs. Most are custom made to one's head size.

Other commercially available wigs include *fake fur* and *yarn wigs*. Wigs worn by some clowns are actually wigs intended for normal use by ladies. Most wigs of this type are colored red, auburn, blonde, or gray. They, like any other wig, need trimming before use. Daisy is wearing a commercial wig in Figure 6-21.

BALD PATES

Wigs which are bald at the crown of the head are called *bald pate* wigs. Jack Anderson is wearing a bald pate afro wig in Figure 5-21. These wigs are similar to the afro, curly, or silly boy — with a cotton or synthetic cloth replacing the hair on top and front of the wig. Normally, the cloth pate is white, a color that works well for the whiteface clown but looks strange on an auguste or tramp clown. To overcome this problem, the cloth or bald pate can be colored with makeup. Use the same color that you apply to your face on the pate, so the bald head and your face will match.

Coloring the Pate
To color the bald pate with greasepaint, place the wig on a stand. Apply the greasepaint to the cloth with your fingers or a makeup sponge. Use the same makeup you use on your forehead so that the colors will match. Make sure that the

Figure 14-1

cloth is thoroughly covered with greasepaint. Be careful to keep makeup off the hair.

After the makeup has been applied, rubbed in and smoothed, apply a heavy coat of powder over the entire pate. Rub it in onto the greasepaint and add a bit more powder. Let the powder set for 24 hours. After the powder has set, remove the excess with a medium to stiff-bristled brush. Powder and brush one more time.

Now take the wig and turn it inside out. If any greasepaint has soaked through the cloth, powder the underside of the pate. After the powder has soaked in and has been brushed off, the wig is ready to be trimmed or styled.

Even though greasepaint has been applied to the pate of a bald wig, the wig can still be washed when it becomes dirty, but it will be necessary to reapply the greasepaint and powder.

WIGS FOR TRAMPS

Should a tramp clown wear a wig? Some tramp clowns say yes, others say no. Both arguments have merit. If a tramp clown has natural hair which is long, shaggy, and stringy enough to give the appearance of a man-of-the-road who is totally unkempt and ungroomed, it is all right to use the natural hair. However, very, very few clowns fit into this category. All others should wear a wig. Nothing looks more out of place than a shabbily dressed, sad faced, tramp clown with a neatly trimmed head of hair.

Wigs for the tramp should be a neutral color such as black, brown, or gray. A tramp clown does not wear a brightly colored wig. It is totally out of character.

Silly boy wigs or bald pate wigs with neutral colored hair are ideal for tramps. The pate, of course, must be covered with makeup to match the face. Many tramp clowns use wigs off the shelf and trim them until they are appropriate to be worn. Homemade wigs of fake fur in neutral color are also appropriate for the tramp.

MAKING YOUR OWN WIGS

Commercial Wigs

If you are not able to find a wig which suits your taste, try a commercially available lady's street wig. If the color of a regular street wig does not suit you, color one. Inexpensive blonde or light gray wigs can be colored with felt-tip markers. The marker must contain permanent ink or the color will run when you perspire or get caught in the rain.

In addition to the wig and marker, you will need a pair of rubber gloves, a pair of pliers, and a small glass or cup of rubbing alcohol. The first step is to put on the gloves to prevent the dye in the marker from staining your hands. The second step is to take the pliers and break the plastic case and remove the felt portion of the marker. The felt strip is saturated with dye. Breaking away the housing allows you to use the entire felt piece to color the wig.

Coat the wig with the dye from the marker. The process is slow and will take an hour or so. The alcohol is used to replace the evaporating solvent in the felt. As the felt begins to dry out moisten it with alcohol. Normally, two felt-tip markers will be required to color a wig.

Once the wig has been colored, let it dry overnight. It must then be trimmed and styled. Felt dyed wigs can be machine washed when needed and have proven to be very durable.

Fake Fur

Fake fur, available at fabric stores, makes relatively inexpensive wigs. They are, however, hot in the summertime. The fake fur wigs can be made several ways. The simplest is to cut a circle of fake fur about six inches in diameter. Cut with a single-edge razor blade rather than a pair of scissors; scissors tend to cut the fur as well as the backing material. After cutting the circle, cut a second piece of fake fur about 19 inches by four inches. Sew one of the 19-inch edges to the outer edge of the circle. Trim the

19-inch segment so the two four-inch ends just meet and then sew them together. This will give the wig the shape of a birthday cake. Finally, sew a thin elastic band on the inside the outer edge of the wig. The fake fur wig is ready to wear.

If there is any doubt about the size of your head and how the wig will fit, make a pattern out of a grocery sack and tape to determine the exact sizes of the two fake fur pieces needed for your wig.

Fake fur can also be attached to a skull cap in order to make a bald fake fur wig. If this wig is worn by an auguste or tramp clown, the pate portion of the skull cap should be colored with greasepaint as described earlier.

Yarn Wigs

Wigs can also be made from yarn. An easy way to make the yarn wig is to use the body portion of a pair of panty hose. Cut off the leg parts of the panty hose and sew the openings shut. After this is done sew loops of yarn onto the panty hose.

If you wear this wig with a hat, you will not need to cover the entire panty hose with yarn, only that portion of the wig showing below the hat.

Trimming

The afro wig requires a great deal of work before it is ready to wear. The first step is to comb or pick the hair on the wig. Once the step is completed, you will have a very large wig with much more hair than you need or want. You must trim it to a manageable length. The trimming should begin at the forehead area. Trim the wig so that your clown eyebrows show. It does not make sense to take time to apply eyebrows and then cover them with a wig which is too long.

As you trim, cut only half of what you feel is necessary in the first trim. Continue trimming the forehead area until you are satisfied with the

length. Put the wig on your head to be sure that the length of the hair on the trimmed wig is what you want.

After trimming the front of the wig, trim the sides. Follow the same procedure as described above.

Once the area around your face has been cut, trim the remainder of the wig. Make sure that the wig is completely combed. If it is not, recomb it and recheck the length of the areas you have trimmed.

The easiest way to trim the remainder of the wig is to place it on a wig stand and begin trimming to the length you want. Take your time. After cutting off excess material from the entire wig, you may need to go back and trim in some areas to make the length uniform.

Once the trimming is complete, the wig should be recombed with a pick comb; then any uneven lengths should be trimmed away. When you are satisfied with the appearance of your wig, shake it thoroughly to remove loose hairs or your wig will shed.

During the trimming, try the wig on repeatedly to make sure you are satisfied with your progress.

If you are not sure of your ability to trim a new wig, take it to a barber or beautician and have it professionally trimmed.

Like the afro, the curly wig also needs to be combed and trimmed before wearing. The process of trimming is similar to that of the afro, although some clowns prefer to use a brush rather than a pick comb.

The silly boy wig, off-the-shelf wigs, and yak wigs all need to be combed or brushed, trimmed and shaped before wearing. You can do this yourself or have it done professionally.

Many wig dealers will comb and trim your wig relatively inexpensively. Unless you know how to properly trim a wig, have it done by a professional barber or hair stylist.

Chapter Fifteen

Gallery of Makeup Examples

This chapter presents a wide variety of clown makeup examples. Interesting examples of each of the three clown types are represented illustrating the contrast in makeup design. All of the clowns pictured have applied their makeup proficiently. Some of these facial designs are very skillfully achieved, others less so.

This gallery serves as a pictorial reference of the many different styles of clown makeup designs and illustrates various wigs and hair styles. It can serve as a valuable guide in creating your own clown face.

Guidelines have been provided in this book to help you create each of the three clown types.

This gallery of photos shows similarities and contrasts in design within and between each of the clown categories. You should be familiar enough with clown makeup design to be able to identify at a glance which clowns are auguste, whiteface, and tramp.

It is a natural tendency for beginning clowns to want to imitate a clown face they find appealing. This is to be discouraged. A facial design serves as a trademark and each clown should develop a unique face. Use the photos in this book as guides and examples, but be creative. Design a clown face that is uniquely yours and fits your own facial features and clown character.

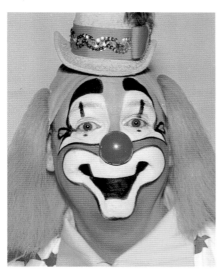

Appendix

Resource Information

CLOWN ORGANIZATIONS

If you would like more information on clown makeup, as well as technique, wardrobe, and general clown instruction, the following organizations provide information through magazine subscriptions, seminars, and workshops which cover all aspects of clowning. Hundreds of local clown groups are afilliated with one or more of these organizations. You can find out more about your nearest local clown group by contacting these organizations.

Clowns International
174 Stockbridge Road
Winchester, Hants. S022 6RW
U.K.

International Shrine Clown Association
1122 Third Avenue
Rockford, IL 61108
U.S.A.

Clowns of America International, Inc.
P.O. Box 6468
Lee's Summit, MO 64064
U.S.A.

World Clown Association
P.O. Box 1413
Corona, CA 91718
U.S.A.

SOURCES OF MATERIALS

Theater, costume, magic and novelty shops carry quality makeup supplies. If your area does not have a clown makeup supplier you can receive a catalog from a number of manufactures and cosmetic dealers. The following firms are sources of theatrical makeup supplies. Some of these companies do not sell directly to customers but they will have a list of merchants who do carry their makeup.

Ben Nye Company, Inc.
5935 Bowcroft Street
Los Angeles, CA 90016
U.S.A.

Bob Kelly Cosmetics, Inc.
151 West 46 Street
New York, NY 10036
U.S.A.

Kryolan Corporation
132 Ninth Street
San Francisco, CA 94103
U.S.A.

Mehron, Inc.
45 E. Route 303
Valley Cottage, NY 10989
U.S.A.

M. Stein Cosmetic Company
10 Henery Street
Freeport, NY 11520
U.S.A.

Wig Creations Ltd.
12 Old Burlington Street
London W1X 2PX
U.K.

Playbill/Ideal Wigs
37-11 35th Avenue
Astoria, NY 11101
U.S.A.

ProKnows
P.O. Box 12
Buchanan, VA 24066
U.S.A.

BIBLIOGRAPHY

Listed below are a few good books that can help further your knowledge of theatrical makeup techniques and clowning skills.

Buchman, Herman. *Stage Makeup*, Watson-Guptill Publications, 1971

Fife, Bruce, et al. *Creative Clowning*, Piccadilly Books, Ltd. 1992

Fife, Bruce, et al. *The Birthday Party Business*, Piccadilly Books, Ltd. 1998

Ginn, David. *Clown Magic*, Piccadilly Books, Ltd. 1993

Jans, Martin. *Stage Makeup Techniques*, Players Press, Inc., 1986

Index

UNIQUE BOOKS FROM PICCADILLY

CREATIVE CLOWNING

Edited and Compiled by Bruce Fife
Foreword by Richard Snowberg,
President World Clown Association

Drawing from the combined experience and talents of eight professional entertainers, the authors provide step-by-step instruction on everything from comedy magic to stilt walking. This book goes beyond merely explaining how to perform the physical skills, it teaches how to use these skills creatively to become funny and entertaining. Includes valuable information on how to work with an audience, how to use props effectively, describes physical comedy techniques, how to create and tell jokes, and even provides complete details on how to set up a profitable clowning business.

"An excellent book...If you're not funnier after reading this book, you're hopeless."
— *The Book Reader*

"For those who are considering a career in clowndom, this book is a must. For those who just want to have a good time reading about this most happy of careers, this book is also a must."
— *Nashua Telegraph*

HOW TO BE A GOOFY JUGGLER
A COMPLETE COURSE IN JUGGLING MADE *RIDICULOUSLY* EASY!
by Bruce Fife

Given the proper instruction *anybody* can learn how to juggle. With this informative guide you will not only learn how to juggle, but you will learn how to make your juggling ridiculously funny. Filled with lots of simple, yet humorous, tricks and snappy one-liners.

"Presented in a bright, witty tone, the book is pure fun...It's easy to read...and will definitely entertain you."
— *The Post Newspapers*

"If you want to do something weird, try *How to Be a Goofy Juggler*...which will make you giggle even if you are as butter-fingered as I am...One thing guaranteed is a great time."
— *Book Bag Reviews*

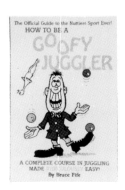

DR. DROPO'S BALLOON SCULPTURING FOR BEGINNERS

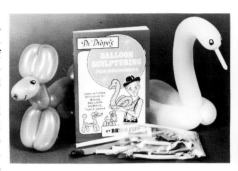

Balloon dogs, birds, camels, and kangaroos. These are just a few of the colorful rubbery animals that can be created out of simple balloons. Used by clowns and magicians to delight and entertain audiences, the art of balloon sculpturing is now available to everyone. In this delightful book Dr. Dropo shares his secrets for making several popular balloon animals, toys, and games.

"Amazing shapes...amusing animals and other figures...It is an unusual hobby for people of any age...recommedned."
— *Booklist (American Library Association)*

"Great fun and it's about time someone gave us a good course in the art."
— *Rainbo Electronic Reviews*

VENTRILOQUISM MADE EASY
HOW TO TALK TO YOUR HAND WITHOUT LOOKING STUPID!
by Paul Stadelman and Bruce Fife

The secrets of ventriloquism revealed! Learn how to throw your voice. Make your hand talk, your shoe sing, and your socks come alive! Everyone, but you, will be tongue-tied when you talk to your socks and they talk back! This book explains how to use standard puppets as well as novelty figures such as balloon animals and sock puppets. Includes 22 complete comedy dialogs to get you started.

"An OUTSTANDING quality job...You present a fresh new look at a very popular form of entertainment." — *Stephen Axtell, Axtell Expressions*

"Wonderful book!...the best resource book currently on the market for the aspiring ventriloquist."
— *Clinton Detweiler, President of The North American Association of Ventriloquists*

These books are available in bookstores and novelty shops. If they are not available in your area you can order them direct from the publisher. When ordering direct, please include $1 for each book to cover postage and handling. Write and ask for a free Piccadilly Books Catalog.

PICCADILLY BOOKS

Distributed by: Empire Publishing Service